Praise for *Rock to Recovery*

"Music has always been how I've gotten through my darkest moments. These stories about the work Rock to Recovery® does proves just how powerful music can be as a healing force for veterans and people who are suffering."

—Jonathan Davis
Singer for the GRAMMY award-winning band Korn

"Page-turning stories from the revolutionary program that is helping lost souls find their voices through music and teamwork."

—Allan Leslie Combs, PhD
CIIS Professor of Consciousness Studies
President Emeritus & Assistant to the VP of
The Society for Consciousness Studies

"For eons music has been employed as a healing balm for those willing to acknowledge its power. *Rock to Recovery* explores the amazing utility of music that many take for granted. It is both inspiring and instructive."

—Aloe Blacc
GRAMMY Nominated Artist

"*Rock to Recovery* has a powerful heartbeat. When one heart tunes in, it can heal the other."

—Eden Sassoon
The Sassoon Way – Beauty & Wellness show on Sway TV,
entrepreneur, Season 7 *Real Housewives of Beverly Hills*

"Rock to Recovery® is an amazing organization that I've supported from day one! This book brings insight to how music really is the universal healer."

—**Shavo Odadjian**
System of a Down, North Kingsley

"One of the fears and/or excuses people have about getting sober is the worry of being bored or becoming boring. Rock to Recovery® shows the vibrancy and excitement that sobriety can rock!"

—**Acey Slade**
Murderdolls, Joan Jett & the Blackhearts, and Dope

"There are few things that transform my darkest moments like music and the arts. *Rock to Recovery* shows how that power can work for anyone."

—**Brandon Lee**
Emmy Award winning journalist,
author *Mascara Boy*, TV news anchor

"Rock to Recovery® uses the power of music to provide healing for people suffering from addiction or trauma through their musical interventions. It's beautiful to witness so many people benefit from their work who have been able to improve self-esteem, self-expression, reduce stress, and facilitate long-term growth and recovery."

—**Erica Krusen, LMFT**
Managing Director, Mental Health &
Addiction Services, MusiCares

"This moving new book will allow Rock to Recovery® to expand their incredible work and bring needed, inspiring stories of recovery to many."

—**Genevieve Morton**
Entrepreneur and *Sports Illustrated* swimsuit model

"I hosted Warrior Care events at Eglin AFB in back-to-back years, and Rock to Recovery® was a centerpiece of the teaming. I saw first-hand the power of music as Wounded Warriors grew in strength and hope. The devotion of Rock to Recovery to this very important cause is inspiring, and America's Airmen continue to thrive thanks to the Rock to Recovery team. You guys Rock!"

—**Maj Gen Chris Azzano**
Air Force Test Center Commander, Edwards AFB, California

"Music can be transformative in many ways; Rock to Recovery® shows how it can help those fighting serious substance problems."

—**Art Rosenbaum**
Folklorist, folk musician, and GRAMMY Winner

"Wes Geer and Constance Scharff's latest book makes a riveting and unique contribution to the ever-important field of addiction and recovery. Based upon their work with Rock to Recovery®, as well as their own personal experiences, Geer and Scharff show clearly and brilliantly, through eighteen well-written testimonies, how the transformative power of music greatly facilitates recovery processes in individuals struggling with various phases of addiction and trauma."

—**Dr. Rony Alfandary**
Clinical Social Worker, Director of the Postgraduate
Psychoanalytic Psychotherapy Programme, Bar-Ilan University, Israel

"*Rock to Recovery: Music as a Catalyst for Human Transformation* is a compelling collection of stories from people who have overcome addiction and trauma. This powerful and deeply moving book will save lives. *Rock to Recovery* anchors its stories to an organization of the same name that brings professional musicians together with folks in recovery to create music. The organization's model of change is to rewire the brain and gives participants an experience of hope and accomplishment through collaborative songwriting. These essays reveal that music really is the medicine. I highly recommend this book for anyone who is struggling to overcome trauma or addiction as it offers a compassionate lifeline."

—**Dr. Caroline Heldman, PhD**
Chair, Critical Theory & Social Justice Department & Chair,
Gender, Women, & Sexuality Studies Minor Occidental College
CoFounder, The Matrix Webinar Series

"Playwright William Congreve was certainly onto something when he wrote, 'Music has charms to sooth a savage breast, to soften rocks, or bend a knotted oak.' Authors Constance Scharff and Wesley Geer are certainly onto something with their Rock to Recovery® program for soothing the savage grip of addiction and trauma. This wonderful guide to using a music immersion program for treating alcoholics, addicts, and trauma survivors is based in science, but it is most powerful when told through its emotional and astonishing stories of recovery."

—**Judy Muller**
Professor Emerita, USC Annenberg School of Journalism,
former ABC News Correspondent,
and Emmy award winning journalist

"Addiction and trauma can sometimes lead to misery, robbing people of their dignity. *Rock to Recovery*'s inspirational stories demonstrate that the power of making music can bring hope, dignity, and recovery. Thank you for sharing them."

—**Professor Gabriel Ivbijaro**
MBE, JP, MBBS, MMedSci, MA, PhD, FRCGP,
FWACPsych, IDFAPA
Secretary General World Federation for Mental Health
President, World Dignity Project
Medical Director, Wood Street Medical Centre, London, England

ROCK TO RECOVERY

MUSIC AS A CATALYST FOR HUMAN TRANSFORMATION

WES GEER AND CONSTANCE SCHARFF, PHD

Rock to Recovery: Music as a Catalyst for Human Transformation

Published by Around The Way Publishing, LLC
21700 Oxnard Street, Suite 660
Woodland Hills, California 91367

ISBN: 978-1-7355299-7-4 (paperback)
ISBN: 978-1-7355299-6-7 (ebook)
ISBN: 978-1-7355299-5-0 (audiobook)

LCCN: 2021913276

Front cover design by Tyler Spangler
Author image by Travis Commeau
Back cover image by Paul A. Hebert

In loving memory of Rock to Recovery brother Christian Heldman and the many we've lost to addiction and trauma. This is for you.

CONTENTS

Active-Duty Military and Veterans
Science Column
Mental Health Issues among Active-Duty Military and Veterans, 189

The Researcher
Science Column
Music and the Brain, 229

FOREWORD

Music can change a person's life. I know because music dramatically changed mine.

I met Wes Geer in Huntington Beach, California, back in '92 or '93. I have many memories of Wes hangin' out at the local downtown bars on Main Street drinking beer, shooting pool, or hitting on girls. I didn't know him particularly well back then, but when he and his friends put together the band Hed PE, I definitely started paying close attention to Wes Geer!

From the very beginning of Hed PE, Wes had something very special going on with his guitar playing that I quickly took notice of. What I remember most was his unique ear for melody and modern guitar pedal techniques, but he also challenged me with the way he mixed in other styles of guitar playing with heavy rock riffs. Blew my mind! Me and my guitar twin, James "Munky" Shaffer from Korn, thought very highly of Wes and Hed PE.

In early 2005, I stepped away from Korn after experiencing a dramatic spiritual awakening. I became obsessively determined to face my addiction issues head on and learn the root cause of them. During my time away from Korn, Wes was hired to join the band. He was chosen because of his incredible talent, but being completely sober was a major deciding factor for the Korn guys as well. They needed someone clean who could show up day after day without any drama. Wes filled that role for years, touring with humility and a strong desire to be of service to Korn as well as our loyal fan base.

Eventually, I returned to the band, which unfortunately meant that Wes was out of a job. I remember the entire experience that led to my return like it was yesterday. I ended up visiting a big festival that Korn was playing, hoping to quietly hang out as a spectator. I was actually excited to see Korn for the first time without me in the band.

But just before the show, I met up with the guys, and Munky ended up asking me to play Korn's very first single, "Blind," with them during their set. For me, it was a magical feeling to be back onstage with my brothers, but for Wes, that night set in motion the beginning of the end of his time with Korn. Feeling a little bit defeated and not knowing what to do with his life at that point, Wes knew exactly who to turn to: God.

What could a middle-aged, out-of-work guitar player do with his life? How could he bring something important to the world and people in need? I respect Wes' reliance upon prayer. My relationship with God has been unfolding over the years, and I credit that bond with getting and staying clean, clear, and sober. My family, relationships with church and friends, and my return to Korn—I'm so thankful to Christ for all of it. Without God, I could have been just another musician gone way too soon.

The answer Wes received to his prayers was the brilliant idea to form Rock to Recovery ®. Rock to Recovery brings the experience of playing in a band to people who are not musicians. What a mind-blowing idea! Bandmates don't always get along. People in bands are just like family, and as we all fully know, families often have many problems to work through in life. But in the end, my bandmates ended up being a powerful support to me. Rock to Recovery gives that experience of connection, a sort of family connection, to people who are in treatment for addiction, mental health problems, or trauma. Everyday people get to have the experience of writing and recording a song, of being part of a band, of hearing their song play on the internet after Rock to Recovery sessions. It's a powerful activity for those who get the opportunity to participate.

I recently got to see Rock to Recovery at work in Nashville. I visited The Next Door, a Christian ministry and addiction treatment facility that helps women overcome addiction, especially pregnant women and those with young children. The Next Door works with passion and commitment to bring opportunities for healing and hope to keep families united and help keep women from falling back into addictive patterns that not only have the potential to kill them but have untold impacts on the children they abandon or leave behind with their incarceration or deaths.

Led by Rock to Recovery's Phil Bogard, whose recovery story is in this book, the women crafted a song that made me want to jam! They poured their souls into the lyrics and sang so sweetly, I thought I might weep. Music alone doesn't cure addiction; but music as a therapeutic tool, as a means to connecting to each other and to God, music in that form has the ability to change lives. I've seen it with my own eyes and lived it in my spirit.

In 2021, there are fifteen musicians who serve Rock to Recovery across four states. They form 500 bands a month, working with 2,500 people. Rock to Recovery even has a contract with

the Department of Defense to provide services to the Air Force
Wounded Warrior (AFW2) program. I am proud of my friend Wes
and his commitment to helping people recover from the problems
they face with their mental health.

Wes is such a talented musician and a brilliant guy. He showed
how smart he is by partnering with Constance Scharff, "Doc," as
the Rock to Recovery family affectionately calls her. She has a PhD
in Transformative Studies and explained her work to me as looking
at how change happens. She focuses her efforts on understanding
how easily accessible interventions, like music, can help people
heal. She understands the science behind why writing and playing
music helps people recover from many different mental health issues. Music doesn't just affect our spirits, Doc will tell you, it also
has a positive impact on our brains.

Doc became interested in mental health treatment when she
saw veterans not receiving the mental healthcare they needed to
recover after returning from Iraq and Afghanistan. She watched
as they relapsed and sometimes succumbed to suicide. Depressed
and suffering from her own trauma, Doc got angry. She was certain that there was better treatment for herself and the veterans she
knew. That's when she dove into the research on complementary
therapies for addiction and trauma recovery. After nearly two decades of work in the field, she was awarded the Sol Feinstone Humanitarian Award from St. Lawrence University for her advocacy
on behalf of those who suffer from addiction and mental health
issues. Her dedication to and love for the work Rock to Recovery
does made her the perfect writing partner for Wes. They are the
right team to share the message of hope contained in this book.

Music has the power to heal. Whether I am writing a song,

playing onstage, or listening to music that moves me, music changes the way I feel, always for the better. Rock to Recovery brings this powerful healing method to people who are at the lowest points in their lives.

Through the eighteen stories shared in this book, you'll learn exactly how music helps us all: the musicians who are program facilitators for Rock to Recovery and the precious souls who have participated and benefited from the Rock to Recovery program. Not everyone makes it. Music is not a miracle cure. Too many people we love continue to die from addiction and suicide. But many do recover, and we can definitely celebrate their triumphs and gather hope and inspiration from their experiences.

We all have the ability to write our own song if we are shown the way. As they say in Rock to Recovery, "Music Is the Medicine!"

—Brian "Head" Welch,
Guitarist for the GRAMMY Award-winning band Korn,
New York Times bestselling author of *Save Me from Myself*,
and costar of the Showtime movie *Loud Krazy Love*

PREFACE

Music has the power to heal. At Rock to Recovery's annual benefit concerts, we quickly sell out our t-shirts that say "I saved my soul with rock n roll." Why? Because almost anyone who has ever listened to music intuitively understands its healing qualities. When we have a bad day, there's music that we reach for to cheer us up. When we're happy, there is music that we associate with joy. Angry? Outraged? Sad? Frustrated? Reminiscing? We each have a personal soundtrack that helps us bring forth and process emotion.

Without other therapeutic interventions, music is not a curative for addiction, trauma, or mental health issues. Writing or singing a song on its own won't magically transform your life. However, music can be a tool that makes a positive difference to treatment outcomes when used in conjunction with other therapies and self-help strategies. Playing music and singing provides openings for emotional expression, upliftment, community connection, and the creation of a feeling of hope in situations that may feel hopeless.

This is a book about hope. At Rock to Recovery®, we sometimes refer to our musicians as "hope slingers." It is the goal of both this book and our programs to create hope and opportunities for change through the healing power of music. Whether the reader has access to the Rock to Recovery program or not, we believe that these stories will show how playing music and singing opens doors to recovery. Each of us can use music to help us change. As poet and musician Leonard Cohen suggested, cracks are how the "light gets in." All of us have cracks. The light that comes in is from the music of our hearts.

This book surveys the experiences of individuals from around the nation who are part of Rock to Recovery, an organization that provides a unique form of music programming to help people recover from a wide range of issues, including trauma, addiction, eating disorders, depression, and other mental health concerns. At the time of publication, Rock to Recovery partners with more than 100 programs in four states and has a contract with the Department of Defense to work with the Air Force Wounded Warrior (AFW2) program and, most recently, the US Navy. We work with youth, veterans, pregnant women, homeless people, LGBTQ+ individuals, drug courts—literally anyone who may benefit from the ways in which music changes neurology and biochemistry, which is anyone with a heart and a brain. The potential application for the Rock to Recovery program is broad and without boundaries.

This book's authors are a guitarist and a mental health researcher who have dedicated their lives to helping people thrive. Wes noticed when he was in rehab that playing guitar and singing with people instantly transformed the energy in the room. Constance is a mental health researcher who helps clinicians choose complementary mental healthcare practices that improve treatment outcomes. We present readers with the best information we have—anecdotal, clinical, and scientific—so that you can make an informed choice about your own or a loved one's recovery. We encourage you to verify anything we share here. There are many paths to wellness. Music is but one treatment tool.

We have chosen to tell the Rock to Recovery story through the experiences of our musicians and participants. These stories are based on recorded interviews. Participants were selected to showcase the widest demographic range possible with regard to age, race and ethnicity, socioeconomic status, diagnosed mental or physical concerns, religion, gender, and sexual orientation. The interviews were recorded, transcribed, and edited for length and fluidity of storytelling. A great effort was made to allow each person interviewed to tell their story in their own words. Because of this, standard forms of grammar, punctuation, and storytelling are sometimes set aside. Each person shares the powerful role that music has played in their lives, specifically how Rock to Recovery has assisted in improving their health and healing.

This book is filled with music. Each chapter has a song chosen as a theme we believe complements the lived experience of each interviewee. We have also showcased five songs written by Rock to Recovery participants and musicians so that the reader gets a feel for the kind of work we do when writing lyrics. Our song catalogue can be accessed on SoundCloud. A link can be found on the Rock to Recovery website.

Interviewees who are participants in Rock to Recovery programs had most identifying characteristics removed from their stories. Despite efforts to eliminate the social stigma associated with addiction, mental illness, and war-related injuries, stigma remains. Most have chosen to use a first name or pseudonym. The professionals and Rock to Recovery musicians who were interviewed for this book have chosen to attach their names to the project. Anonymizing our stories would diffuse their impact. Wes and Constance, for example, want you to know that not only could we recover from addiction and mental health issues, but we also went on to live wonderful lives. We want the reader to verify the authenticity of the stories we share.

Although research studies on Rock to Recovery are forthcoming, this book chooses a creative nonfiction format. We believe there is value in providing a forum for program participants to share their experiences in their own words. It is our assertion that the facilitators' and participants' perspectives about what they have gained from being involved with Rock to Recovery are profound and provide a different point of view than an academic study. However, researchers who would like to do an efficacy study on Rock to Recovery, please contact us. A core part of our mission is to help further the knowledge and understanding of music, in its varied forms, as a therapeutic offering. Rock to Recovery welcomes opportunities to work with academics who want to help us improve mental health through music programming.

Our greatest hope in writing this book is that you will be inspired. Music has been used in healing and ritual for thousands of years. It was our pleasure to be able to talk with some of Rock to Recovery's participants to find out how they have experienced the program and to learn firsthand the ways in which "music is the medicine." If you or someone you know suffers from addiction, mental illness, trauma, or other issues, we are confident that you will hear in these stories of recovery that there is treatment and hope. Join our community. We can be reached online and do our best to respond to all inquiries.

1

WES GEER

"Little Dreamer" by Van Halen

For the addicted, I truly believe that there seem to be two voices that we have inside us. When I'm getting loaded, the one voice keeps saying, "Get loaded," and I have no power to resist. I know the other voice is in there, but it's just a murmur. That voice deep inside of me that knows I should stop can't get through.

With me, it was like my whole life I wanted people to like me. I wanted to fit in, but I couldn't figure out how. And we moved a lot. I'd make some friends, and my family would move, so there the friends went; then I'd have to start over. But when I was around fourteen, I discovered the guitar, and being a new kid in a new city, the guitar became my best friend.

It seemed like I always connected quickest with the guys hanging out on the bleachers with the ripped jeans and the weed. Soon, weed and guitar were my favorite pastimes.

I grew up surrounded by classical music. So, I remember vividly the day when my brother played "Smoke on the Water" on acoustic guitar. That cutting-rock sound always stuck with me. I had to learn how to make those sounds. I was obsessed; so, like any other kid in high school dreaming of being a rock star, I created a band with a couple of my friends.

When we were young and got some of our first albums, like Dead Kennedys or Iron Maiden, the imagery was freaky, even scary, but we loved it. We spent all our money buying spiked wristbands, parachute pants, and vinyl. We were fully invested in the rock star fantasy.

We'd got a look at some of the pictures on the rock albums— like Mötley Crüe's first record—and the guys in the band looked like freaks, so we wanted to look like that. Ripped jeans. Sleeveless t-shirts with skulls and axes and lightning on them. I wanted long hair, but my parents didn't buy into the dream as fully as I did, and my hair stayed pretty short. Still, we fully bought into the rock star fantasy, and the weed helped because, really, we sucked.

We had my guitar and a kids' Mickey Mouse drum set we found in the neighbor's trash. The drummer was the first guy to turn me on to weed. When I was stoned, everything I played sounded so friggin' amazing, at least to me. Getting high and playing guitar for hours was my favorite thing to do, and I did it a lot. The places it took me were otherworldly.

When I would smoke some weed, I'd go into these four-hour holes—I called them my weed holes. I filled them with playing guitar. I'd play for hours and come out to say, "Wow! What just happened?" I loved getting lost in those weed-and-music-induced time warps, and I loved the progress I was making on my instrument, so I went back again and again.

I wanted to be stoned all the time. I had the bright idea to smoke in the boys' bathroom between classes, and I got caught.

That got me kicked out of school. To avoid having to go to the local continuation school "where they send the rejects," we decided it would be best for me to move in with my dad and stay in a "normal" high school. Instead of a tragedy, I saw this as an opportunity to finally grow my hair out. I didn't even consider quitting weed. The "get loaded" voice had free rein at my dad's. I kept smoking weed and ditching school constantly, and I ended up in a continuation high school after all. Finally, Dad tightened the screws so hard I had to show up. One random day in October, I was called to the office. I'd graduated, and high school was suddenly over.

After that, I moved into my car because I had started using cocaine and not coming home. I signed up for college and didn't go. My dad got so sick of worrying that I was dead every night, he kicked me out. I got a job at Domino's Pizza just to survive.

My mom decided to try to help. She hadn't given up on me, and I had graduated, after all. So she helped me get a job at the company she worked at, an insurance company. I did well. I excelled there, probably because for a while I put down the weed. I worked my way up from data entry to managing the data intake division.

That was in the '80s, and there was always a band. Bands I played in came and went, and none of them were very good. During that time, I was drinking. I drank a lot on weekends—tequila and pitchers of beer. Though I was playing in shitty bands and drunk a lot, I thought my life was pretty good.

One day at work, I was changing desks—I don't remember why—and I'm emptying my drawers and I found all these fliers I'd made for all the various bands I'd been playing with. It made me go, like, "Are you an idiot? None of these bands have amounted to much. Maybe you should just give this up." But I didn't listen to that voice. Even though I had a great job, especially for somebody with barely a high school education, I couldn't imagine myself stuck forever in the cubicle life. I knew my only way out of there was to hang on to this dream of being a rock star.

By then it was the early '90s. I saw that the music scene in LA was dying. The glam days were over, and Seattle hadn't hit yet. I was searching for the next big scene. I didn't want to give up on the dream.

I looked around and picked Huntington Beach. Everything was hitting down by the beach. I told the band I was playing with at the time, "We gotta get down to the beach. That's where it's at. I can feel the vibe down there." And we went. Snowboarding was blowing up. Skateboarding was making a comeback. There were a bunch of clubs, and they would all have a band play and then a DJ spin disco all night. It was a killer scene.

Then the band I'd been in broke up. That was OK because I had been putting together a better lineup, and this one had potential. This became Hed. That was '94, and bands like Red Hot Chili Peppers, Nine Inch Nails, Jane's Addiction, Alice in Chains, and Nirvana were rewriting the world of music. They were all redefining the industry. The next chapter was here.

I felt like I needed a muse, that magic ingredient to push us over the top. I came home drunk one afternoon and stumbled in on my roommates snorting meth. I joined them. The meth woke me out of a stupor just in time for rehearsal, so of course I thought, "This is amazing!" I wrote two songs in the car en route to the jam room. My meth use accelerated my alcoholism exponentially. I felt like I'd found the magic elixir I'd been looking for.

I was a visionary for the band. I thought I owed it to the meth. Hed was my baby, and I was on fire. For a while, that worked. I was cultivating our look, our sound, and I was writing a ton of music. I even got into poetry with my singer, Jared, and convinced him to start rapping. We were all getting loaded like crazy, but we were brothers. We were making magic.

Hed was playing shows with great bands like Incubus, Deftones, Snot, and Korn, and we were getting noticed by the record labels. A&R guys were flying in to see us play in places like Yorba Linda. I was using meth daily and drinking more and more, but it wasn't like I saw the "get loaded" voice as any kind of problem. I mean, Jive Records was flying out to see us! We were crushing it. I had the respect of my band. We had a huge buzz. People loved us. And there were always a lot of drugs in the music scene. I got loaded every day, and I thought those days were magic. We were flying.

But there was a price to be paid. We were doing a tour—a major tour—with System of a Down and Slipknot. They were really big. I was still smoking weed along with the meth, and I thought I was doing great. We were playing a gig in San Bernardino, and my manager came to the show to support us. It'd been a while—we mostly just used the phone to talk—and when he saw me, his eyes bugged out. He said, "Jesus Christ, Wesley. Next stop Auschwitz or what?" I didn't realize how strung out I looked. I was 123 pounds on a six-foot-one frame. I thought I was OK.

But I did know I didn't want my mom to see me because I never came down from the meth. I couldn't. I didn't want to. I told my folks I was in a successful band and really busy. Really, though, I couldn't let them see how sucked up I was. I couldn't lay off it long enough to even drop by. I was hiding from my family and staying loaded.

Then my mom got diagnosed with breast cancer. I don't even remember how I found out about it; I was so loaded all the time. I hadn't seen her in a while, and she was in the hospital. I wanted to see her, but at the same time, I didn't want her to see me. I wanted to be with my mom, but I was a drug addict and couldn't get myself to show up. She could've been dying for all I knew, but I couldn't face the severity of the situation. Honestly, I was in complete denial. It's like I blocked the entire notion out of my brain. And since I couldn't stop using, I did the least possible; I showed up only on the last day she was at the hospital. I stayed in her room a few minutes, and then I had to go. I didn't think about that for a long time, but I know the shame was there, buried in my numbed-out soul.

Somehow I let go of meth for a while, and we had the greatest success ever. Hed made the best record of our careers, and it charted higher than anything we'd ever done before. We had a million-dollar budget and even got a video on rotation on MTV. But less meth meant more drinking and everything else.

Hed started falling apart. Like so many bands, the breakdown began because of a woman, and the choices I made as a sick, lonely, loaded person. No matter how hard I tried to own my indiscretion and repair the relationship with my best friend and singer, it just got worse and worse. The last year with the band was hell. I was getting the brutally silent treatment. My friend was avoiding me at all costs, and that's hard to do when you're living on a forty-five-foot tour bus ten months a year.

After months of misery, he exploded and screamed some things that I won't repeat here, but let's just say we'd crossed a point of no return. That was our breaking point. We were in San Antonio, Texas. We were opening up for Godsmack. After that show, I left my baby. I was like, "I'm outta here." I had finally given up on bringing us back together. But I didn't realize how much I identified with that band as my career. We'd been playing together for ten years, and I blew it up. I left in the middle of a tour. My time with Hed was done.

I was terrified about how I was gonna survive, so I called my brother for a job. He had a company and brought me on. He'd let me work there, maybe even become a principal. But I was emotionally destroyed from losing Hed. I dealt with my sadness by going back to meth and adding heroin. After a year of bizarre and erratic behavior, I came clean with my brother and told him about my drug problem. We made a deal. He said, "Get off the hard stuff, and everything will be OK. Keep using, and I'm going to have to let you go." I said, "I'm gonna quit." I thought it'd be no biggie. I could do it myself. I meant I'd give up meth and heroin and just drink and smoke some weed. To me, that was doable.

But my addiction was raging. One night, I was home, and I was dope sick because I didn't have any drugs left. There was a guy staying at my place who was messy when he shot up, got heroin all over the place, but he wouldn't share it with me. So I took a shot glass to the bathroom with me, and I wet my finger and tried to pick up all the smudges that were all over the tile and put them in the shot glass. When I found a couple of brown smears on the tile floor that wouldn't stick to my finger, I got down on that disgusting floor and licked them up, hoping they would make me feel better. Then I took what was in the shot glass and snorted it. By that point, it wasn't about being high; it was about not being dope sick anymore.

My brother had been drug testing me, and of course I failed.

He and another brother had an impromptu intervention with me. I was fired. I had two choices: go to rehab and I might get my job back or go on my merry way.

I agreed to go to a treatment center, and I went all in. When I first got there, I was in such bad shape that the nicest thing anyone ever called me was "Wes the mess." But I was ready to change. When you're in your addiction, you don't care about all the things you love, and by the time I went into rehab, I thought I didn't care about the guitar anymore. But in rehab, one little guitar chord changed my day. I started writing songs again, silly songs that I'd play for the other guys at the center. It brought us together, and that stuck with me. Somehow the music quieted the "get loaded" voice and started to let the other voice get through, and that one was saying, "You're destroying your life." I got clean.

I was working for my brother again and was now engaged. But after a couple years of sobriety, I stopped working the program that let me stay clean, and my life became a disaster again. At first, I thought I could just drink and not use drugs. I wanted to show everyone I could control my drinking. When I broke up with my fiancé, I started to use drugs again. Everything spiraled out of control. I was trying to control my using, but I was drinking every night. One night, I ran into an old friend, and he had meth and heroin. I went back to the stuff—only this time, I was really aware that I was miserable. The pain was on a soul level, and I called my old sponsor from when I was in treatment. He picked me up and took me to a meeting. I remember nodding off the whole time because I was still high.

I knew I didn't have to go back to treatment. I already knew what I had to do; they'd taught it to me when I was in rehab. I reached for the strength to go through the steps again. I asked myself, "What would be different this time?" I challenged myself to never stop doing the program. I connected more deeply with the sober fellowship. Out of desperation to quell the demons in my mind, I started meditating, big time.

For a while, I made peace with the fact that as a sober person, I would probably never play in a band again. But I noticed a painful gnawing in my gut when I went to shows. I wanted to play, and my time onstage was not done. This was not my ego but my soul calling me to play music again.

I realized how much Hed had meant to me, and so I started asking for what I wanted during my meditation. I wanted to be in a band again. Ten days after I asked for that, out of nowhere, I got a text from Korn saying, "Hey, you wanna come play guitar with us?" Fuck, yes, I did! It took a long while to secure that gig. But after several months of doing things way out of my comfort zone and chasing them all over the country, I finally got it. And I bawled like a baby. I played with Korn from 2009 to 2013.

The coolest part for me was getting to tour the world with Korn, totally sober. That whole gig, to me, was a testament to sobriety—if I put my recovery first, incredible things would come to pass. I began to realize that music was my gift from God. I felt like I'd stolen that gift from myself when I turned my back on the guitar for the drugs, and now it was like, "Wow, look what happens to the music when you do this recovery stuff!" I used to think I couldn't be a musician without the drugs, and here I was with the best gig of my life, and a better musician—clean.

It was a paradigm shift. I recognized that drinking and using were killing me, and not doing what was killing me of course made me better. It was like I found a new place in the world, the right place, where I finally fit better than I ever had before.

When the Korn gig was ending, I was terrified. I had a high school education and was a sober musician out of work. I had no idea what to do or where to go, so I turned back to meditation, which I saw as my only hope.

At this point, I was teaching music part time at Fusion Academy. I was asking the universe, "How do I help people and make a living doing it?" That turned out to be the critical question, and it made me see that music wasn't just my gift; it was the gift I could give other people.

I thought giving straight guitar or drum lessons was kind of boring, so instead, we'd write a song. I found this much more engaging. Together, we could write a couple of parts and move between them. Songwriting became not just something I did but something I could do with other people, even non-musicians. That was the birth of Rock to Recovery®.

There hadn't been any music in treatment when I was in rehab. I thought back to what the guitar had done for me and the other guys when I was learning about recovery, and I began to feel called. My new place in the world opened up. I knew what I was supposed to do, and that was bring music to junkies and alkies despairing in rehab, like I had been. I founded Rock to Recovery on 12/12/12. Sorta mystical.

My whole life, back to when I was a kid looking for how I fit in, everything had seemed transitory. For the first time, with Rock to Recovery, I knew this was where I was supposed to be. I knew from experience that you don't have to be a musician for music to help you recover from addiction. I knew that music could be used for healing. I started to bring music into addiction treatment centers. The results were amazing.

One of the first sessions I gave, a guy I call Mr. Pink came late, and he was like, "I'm a junkie. I'm probably gonna die. Why am I in this stupid music session? I'm dope sick. I can't sleep. I can't eat. F' this." I told him, "I totally get it. I've been in your place. This is a new group, trying to use the magic of playing music to help people just like you." I explained we were all writing a song together about our challenges as drug addicts. I got him to buy in. "Do you think you can just give us a try? Here's a shaker." It was a pink egg; it looked like a baby rattle. I told him what we'd been doing, and then we started working on our song. He got engaged. He asked, "How many times does the chorus go? How many times does the verse go?" And by the end, he's jumping up and down, and he's like, "I don't feel dope sick. This was so amazing!" And I'm thinking to myself, "Holy moly."

Not only did music make him forget his physical pain, but it totally transformed him from super dark and not wanting to live to feeling measures of wellness, hope, and connection—with a shaker. I had this sense of fulfillment, of rightness. It felt really good. It's challenging because in a treatment center, there are a bunch of people in dark places, and I'm going in there to engage them and be a leader. It helped build my self-esteem back up, and it gave me a sense of purpose.

There are seemingly endless losses. Chester Bennington was one. He played in our first Rock to Recovery show in 2016, and he truly got what the program was all about. Chester was the lead singer of Linkin Park, and we had toured together way back in the day. There were times in the back of the bus when we'd jam all night and talk about writing songs together, but Linkin Park got huge, and I left the business for a while, so we lost touch. Later on, we were both sober, and then I heard rumors that he might be using. I wasn't sure if they were true, but I remember thinking, "God, I wish I could get to Chester." We sober folks have a special connection and way to support each other that other "normal" people don't have. When he played the Rock to Recovery show, we barely had a moment to connect. As he was walking out the door, I almost didn't say anything but decided instead to fight through the sea of people to say, "Chester, thanks so much for coming." He said, "I love you, Wes" and gave me a big kiss on the cheek. That was the last time I saw him. Not long after, I heard he'd died. It fucking hurts. It could've easily been me. Somehow I'm still here.

Being in recovery and feeling like it's a miracle to even be alive, I am inspired to help others suffering like I used to. I had the magic of this new program, Rock to Recovery, that I've witnessed transform the darkest souls into bright beings. Losing people in droves every day made me even more devoted to helping as many people as I can, as *we* can, via Rock to Recovery.

There's nothing like playing onstage in a legendary rock band to eighty thousand screaming fans. Nothing like it. But for me, the world of being a rock star came with a feeling of "Where's the next check coming from? Will the next tour even come? Will this gig last? Do you like my new record?" Never mind the limitless pool of egos and weirdness. I was endlessly searching for the next paycheck or accolade to help me survive until that song, tour, or interview. And God bless all my friends still out there touring, but with how this industry is now, we can't make any money unless we are touring. I feel like so many of my musician brothers and sisters are sentenced to a life on the road. With all the "glamour" comes an incredible amount of dirt and sacrifice, being away from family, and always trying to keep up with your last success. But for how long?

With Rock to Recovery, I have learned that music can still be in my life, but instead of bringing feelings of scarcity and desperation, music brings fulfillment like I have never before experienced. In the music industry, I was always looking for what I could get: money, fame, attention, respect. Even after amazing experiences like playing in front of those eighty thousand fans and traveling the world, I was forever wanting. Now I have a place in the world. I am filled up on a daily basis as I am touched and moved by the transformations of the people we meet and work with. It's the sober voice now that speaks the loudest, and it screams of gratitude for the gift of the work that we get to do.

MUSICIANS

What Is Rock to Recovery?

Rock to Recovery as an Organization

Rock to Recovery is a pair of sister companies—for-profit and nonprofit—that provide an ancillary service to various types of mental health or addiction treatment facilities. We are part of the weekly curriculum of more than one hundred organizations. We work face to face with people in four states (California, Oregon, Washington, and Tennessee) and nationally through online services. We have a contract with the Department of Defense to serve the Air Force Wounded Warrior (AFW2) program, which we do by traveling to events around the nation and sometimes internationally. For programs outside of our current service area, we can bring intensive workshop experiences to all sorts of groups, from companies looking for team- or leadership-building experiences to youth programs or schools and treatment facilities. Because we are an ancillary service, we are able to provide programming to a wide variety of groups that do not need or could not afford a full-time musician on their staff. Our partnerships allow us to serve approximately 2,500 people each month, thirty thousand people a year.

While our primary work is collaborating as a program partner with treatment facilities, we also provide services to individuals through our weekly online programs. These services are donation based so that anyone who has the desire can participate. Most of the people who are part of our online groups are in recovery, but a growing number are the friends and family of individuals in recovery. For these online groups, musical instruments are not required. The songwriting process uses online production software with virtual instruments in lieu of physical keyboards, drums, and guitars. We also hold meditation groups online, including guided meditation, breathwork, and mindfulness. For individuals who cannot go to treatment because of their work or who need added support after leaving treatment, another company, R2R Companions, provides recovery coaching and sober companion services.

There is a range of cost for services. For nonprofit groups, we provide our music groups at a reduced price. If grant funding is available, we can provide those services for free. Each year, we hold an annual benefit concert in Los Angeles for a dual purpose: to raise funds to comp our services to nonprofit groups that could not otherwise afford a service like ours and to provide an experience of a sober concert to people in recovery. Half of the people in the audience are bussed in from rehab. In all we do, our efforts are to bring music, recovery, and hope to people in need.

Description of a Rock to Recovery Music Session

Rock to Recovery sessions take slightly different forms depending on the group and its needs, but in general, they share a similar format.

Participants walk into a room that is set up for band practice. There will be all sorts of equipment, including a microphone, keyboard(s), hand drums or other percussion instruments, and a guitar or two. The group leader is a professional musician with at least a year of sobriety, though the average at the writing of this book is closer to seven years clean. All of our musicians are in abstinence-based recovery programs. These professionals also have a host of personal qualities that include, but are not limited to, enthusiasm and compassion. We look for sober musicians who have a heart for helping people at the darkest points of their lives.

Participants are welcomed into the room. The program administrator will tell the group a little about themselves, their recovery story, and the history of Rock to Recovery. They will then pose a check-in question. This question or topic is recovery related. What is an area in which you want to grow in your recovery? How do you process anger now that you are sober? Each person in the group shares on the topic for a few minutes. Often, this information is scribed so that it can become part of the lyrics for the song. Those who are having a rough day have an opportunity to share that. As each person closes their share, the whole group says, "You're rad!" and makes a great deal of noise and commotion to celebrate each participant.

After the check-in, the group gets to work writing a song. The first order of business is choosing the type of music they want to create. Rock, rap, reggae, country, etc. are options. The group often chooses the type of music based on the tone of the check-in and the direction the lyrics might go.

Participants are assigned to or volunteer for different parts of the song's creation, from percussion to keyboards to singing. Lyricists get right to work in one corner, writing in a notebook or on a whiteboard. Singers are usually part of the lyric-writing group.

Someone will pick up a guitar. One or two people are assigned to the keyboard. Others take percussion. The band begins to take form.

Individuals work on their own parts in what might seem like controlled chaos, while the group leader assists each section of the band. Because most of the participants have no musical training, this assistance might include some fundamentals of how to play the keyboard or guitar. The leader will generally play lead guitar as a binding element for the group.

By the end of the session, which runs from one to two hours, the group will have written a song. Just before the session closes, the group does a run-through of the song. They then choose a name for it and a band name. Once those elements have been decided, the song is performed and recorded live. Later in the evening, the song is published onto the web, complete with album cover, where it can be shared among participants.

Sounds simple, right? Get a bunch of dope-sick or traumatized non-musicians together for band practice and write a song in about an hour. Although it might seem like an impossible undertaking, we've recorded more than twenty thousand songs to date. It really works.

The magic of the program is in the creative expression in play. Songwriting is a tool to reach specific clinical outcomes. Playing music literally acts organically in a similar way as psychiatric medications do, activating the release of serotonin and dopamine.[1] Singing, which is perhaps the most important part of a session, also releases oxytocin, the love molecule.[2] Participants often feel high at the end of a session because of these changes in neurochemistry.[3]

Rock to Recovery is not a program to teach music or for the treatment of musicians. Rather, it uses the power of music to help those in need to have an experience of hope and accomplishment that will carry them through other aspects of the treatment process.

Working with Non-Musicians

Rock to Recovery's participants are everyday people, most of whom have little or no musical training. A few may be hobbyist musicians. Only a tiny percentage have significant musical skill. Some will have taken up the recorder in grammar school or sung at church or with scout groups at campouts. Others might have dabbled a bit as youngsters before their attention turned to sports or other hobbies. Some might have played in high school band or had piano lessons, which is a helpful addition to any group. A high percentage admit to singing in the shower or the car—after all, who doesn't love to create their own "carpool karaoke" now and again? Lack of musical training, knowledge, or perceived talent is no impediment to successful participation in the Rock to Recovery program.

Music appreciation is universal. Rock to Recovery session leaders don't ask participants whether or not they like music but rather what kind of music they listen to most often. Finding out the type of music participants enjoy allows the group to develop their creativity and build a team concept around a common sound and rhythm. The project of writing a song is the same whether the music chosen is hip hop, country, metal, Bollywood, or show tunes.

The program is specifically designed to allow those without musical training to be successful. It doesn't take years of practice to use personal experience to come up with a lyric or shake a tambourine. Although new participants sometimes balk at the suggestion of the program because they have no musical training, they very quickly realize that it is their ideas and willingness to try something that are desirable.

Although music is written in the sessions, Rock to Recovery is not a program in musicianship. Our mission is to help people heal and transform their lives through the powerful experience of writing, playing, and performing music as a group. The program's emphasis is on providing a creative outlet through which those suffering from mental illness, addiction, or trauma can give voice to their emotions in a cooperative environment and create and finish something of which they can be proud. Music is a tool used to serve that goal. The program was begun with those in treatment for addiction, individuals who are not accustomed to finishing tasks, creating anything beautiful, or feeling proud of a job well done. Those outcomes are not dependent on musical ability. Writing a song is a conduit to remove the obstacles limiting creative expression.

In this section, you will read the experiences of five of our musicians, what brought them to Rock to Recovery, and how being hope slingers has changed their lives. Only four of them are still with us. Music is transformative, but not everyone recovers.

2

SONNY MAYO

"Reach Down" by Temple of the Dog

I believe that we human beings are actually made of music. Think about a violin. There's a reason they call it playing your heart strings, you know? We have heartbeats. We have vocal cords. We have vital organs. When people say, "Let's play it by ear," they are talking about the musicality of our ears. We have eardrums. We *are* music. We are musical instruments. We're meant to make music. We're meant to be musical. I think I've felt that musicality of being my whole life.

That's one of the reasons I am so proud to work with Rock to Recovery because the people I meet in our sessions don't know there's so much music inside them. I'll say, "Hey, will you come over here and learn this bass line on the keyboard?" And they go, "Oh, no, no. I can't. I can't. I don't have any musical…" fill in the blank. And I say, "Well, would you give it a try?" Then I show them a simple bass line or maybe something more complex. Maybe I give them a little extra because they're like, "Whoa! I'm actually doing this."

As they start to learn the thing and they start to nail it, and feel the tempo, combined with the motor action of hitting the correct key and the right note, and having the feel and the execution of expression, they look at me and say, "Oh my God, dude. I got it." I smile because that sense of accomplishment is one of the first of many such good feelings. But I don't say that. Instead, I say, "Yeah. It's not rocket science. It's just rock-and-roll."

Rock-and-roll was my dream when I was growing up in Virginia. As far as I can remember, I have always been moved by and drawn to music. The first record I really remember moving me when I was about seven was "Tracks of My Tears" by Smokey Robinson and the Miracles. It was a little 45 record, and Smokey Robinson pushed me to a point where I was in tears. When I heard that song, there was a yearning in my soul that—well, hearing all that sadness felt good. I liked the hurt. I understand hurt. One of the things I like to share about me is I sensed that I was born sad and melancholy. Trying to live with that undying sadness would feed my addiction later in life.

My first instrument was the viola. I was maybe ten years old, and I had asked for a violin. The person handing out the instruments said, "This is shaped like a violin. Here." It turned out I actually had a viola, which is a sort of a baritone violin, like a violin's older, huskier brother.

In eighth grade, I was diagnosed with osteomyelitis, a painful bone disease. I had it in my left ankle. I was in the hospital quite a bit, and I was lucky I was able to keep my leg. My parents got divorced around this time too. Both the breakup of my family and the disease were traumatic. Bone pain is intense, but I was given a lot of pain medicine, high-powered sedatives. I hadn't messed around with anything addictive, except music, before the bone disease. After my time in the hospital, my relationship with drugs was different. I knew they worked at killing all sorts of pain. In eighth and ninth grades, I went through a "normal" progression of substance use for a budding addict. I stole from my dad's liquor cabinet. I started smoking weed. I don't remember too much of my early drug use though. It fades into the background. What I do remember about that time was starting to play guitar. I was introduced to Metallica, Scorpions, Mötley Crüe, AC/DC, Kiss, Dokken, and, of course, Zeppelin and Hendrix. Those guys were players; those fuckers could play.

Meanwhile, my grandfather was a Pentecostal preacher who believed that rock was the devil's music and gave a seminar on backward, satanic messages in music. He picked on all the stuff that I listened to. I thought that I was going to hell, and I had terrible, traumatic nightmares about demons and burning in hell. I literally felt like demons were all around me, but I didn't see the same evil in the music my grandfather did. I finally just kind of came to terms with the nightmares and said out loud to my fears, "OK. If you guys are gonna hang out, then let's hang out. Fuck it."

I had a sort of spiritual split. I hated my grandfather's God, the God who hated my music, but I have never been a Satanist. I love puppies. I love art. I love music. I love. Period. I'm a gentle guy, and I love connection. Connection is probably what I would call my Higher Power. The high that I get through connecting with people is what drives me, what gives me strength. Relating to other people with love gives me energy and substance.

But at that point, my life turned dark; I was maybe sixteen and getting into trouble. I was a bona fide delinquent. I had been smoking weed and taking acid. Because of that, my mom was making me take surprise urinalysis tests. She would just drop into school, pick me up, and take me to the doctor to get a piss test. I was constantly failing the tests. When I failed, my mom said, "I have to go after what's important to you," and she cut my hair. I had really long hair. I was a full thrash-metal, headbanger kid. I still smoked weed and drank and came up dirty on piss tests. After cutting my hair didn't get the results she wanted, she raised the stakes. "I'm gonna take away your guitars." But while playing music and jamming with my band was real important to me, I still failed the tests. That's the power of addiction, and I was already an addict in high school.

I was sixteen years old in 1987. I came home one night drunk, high, and hallucinating on acid. I basically told my mom I was the messiah. Really. I said, "Sit down, Mom. I have so much to tell you" and proceeded to say to her, "I have a message" and the only way she could really understand what I was trying to say was if she were to liken me to the Messiah.

The next day, I was in rehab.

Back then, in Arlington, Virginia, where I was in treatment, I was not allowed even to touch a guitar. The treatment center considered playing a guitar, especially metal, "drug-related behavior." Playing music was considered the same thing as doing drugs. Thirty years changes a lot of things. Now I bring guitars into rehabs. That feels like such a parallel. I was not allowed to touch a guitar in rehab, and now I bring guitars into rehab and teach people how to play them.

I was in treatment in 1987 for six weeks. It did nothing for me. Nothing. I was biding my time. I heard someone say, "Fake it 'til you make it." I said, "OK." That was something I could do. I was literally going to fake it until people thought I was doing great, and then I was going to do what I do, which was get drunk.

After six weeks, when I got out, I did what I wanted; I did controlled drinking. I mean, again, we're talking about an eleventh-grade kid. I wasn't interested in getting clean. I eventually got sober at thirty, and that is relatively young to get sober. A lot of people go way deeper, use longer. I started young, but in my early twenties, I had no idea about the devastation drugs and alcohol were going to bring to my life. It took fourteen more years for me to hit bottom.

Between sixteen and twenty-three, which is when I moved to California, I had periods when everything was kind of OK. I definitely had problems with drinking and using, but I somehow kept it together enough to have a band that was relatively successful in the DC area. The problem was we were thrash metal, and there was no market for it. During that time, a friend got me a temporary gig with the band Wrathchild America for a few shows. This was the pivotal moment where I took a big step in my career. I had to learn fifteen songs in six days. This became my bread and butter. It's why I have played in so many bands, because I can learn music very quickly.

North Carolina, South Carolina, Florida. Wrathchild America played these big shows, like for one thousand people, and I felt right at home. I said to myself, "Yeah. This is my shit right here. I have no problem doing this. This is exactly what I'm supposed to do." I had always wanted to rock out, always wanted that feeling of being onstage, and I got to experience it. From then on, I had to be in music.

Some friends and I started a band called Mother Fucking Pit

Bulls, or MF Pit Bulls, and started writing music together. In the early '90s, one of the guys got a gig with Ugly Kid Joe and moved to Santa Barbara. When he left, I said to him, "Bro, if you know anybody who needs a killer guitar player, man, I'm ready, dude." He was like, "Cool, man. Be ready."

Easter Sunday 1995, the phone rings, and I answer it. Someone on the other end of the phone says, "Sonny, I've been trying to get ahold of you all day." I ask, "What do you want?" He says, "I want metal." I said, "Bro, you called the right place!" I have never before or again heard such a howl of delight! He said, "Dude, this is Lynn from Snot, and, man, we want you to join our band," and I was all, "Fuck yeah!" He then handed the phone to everybody in the band. The call ended with my friend Tumor, who said, "The guys want a second guitar player. They saw videos of you. They want you."

I left for Santa Barbara right away, and when I pulled up, we went straight to band practice. Snot became a successful band. We had a deal with Geffen Records within a year, but we were volatile together. I discovered crystal meth, and it amped up my insanity. I did all the things that go along with the drug addict who has everything at his disposal: women, sex, drugs, rock-and-roll. It was fantasy and horror rolled together. Thankfully, the three years I spent with Snot didn't kill me. Sadly, addiction did take the life of Lynn Strait, our lead singer.

I had a really good friend in Amen, and I auditioned for that band. I was high on crystal meth during the audition, but, fortunately, they didn't want clean playing. They were like, "Can you get sloppier? Because it's punk rock, don't you know?" I said, "Yeah. Yeah, I can do that." I got the gig.

See, here's the thing. The bands change, but my party situation was moving in one direction: down. I was squatting in Hollywood. I didn't contribute much to the band. I couldn't control my using except on tour. I'd barely even drink then. When I was on tour, I was on my best behavior. I did the reverse of a lot of people, who go nuts on the road. I was smoking crank for four days straight at home, and then I would detox on tour and be 100 percent the solid guy on the road. But when we were in LA, Amen came close to firing me. I got ultimatums: "You can't do this and be in this band at the same time."

I hit bottom at the end of 2001. I was coming off meth. I was being a degenerate junkie, crashing in the apartment of the woman who is now my second ex-wife, with my stuff piled in the middle of her living room under a blanket. She was like, "I can't take this anymore. Get out. Your dog can stay, but you've got to go."

A sober friend who had lovingly attempted to help me recover had suggested I call 411 when I was ready for help. She told me that it was a number I would not forget, and she was right. I asked for a well-known twelve step program. The operator gave me the number for their central office. The lady who answered said, "Go now. There's a meeting starting in a few minutes near you. Hang up the phone and go now." I did. Thankfully, it was a small meeting, five or six people. When they got to me to share, I said, "My name's Sonny, and I don't know—I can't do this anymore. I don't know what to do. I can't stop. I need help."

I was really desperate. I realized I didn't know how to continue, but I didn't know how to stop. I went on tour to Australia to play the Big Day Out when I had eighteen days clean. I didn't know it at the time, but I had been placed in a position of neutrality. I was scared to say it, but the obsession had been removed. I prayed the alcoholic's prayer: "Please help me. I'll do anything to not have to drink and use again today. Please help me." And then somehow, I stayed sober.

This was important when I was on tour, where I was around my old friends from other bands. They were doing their thing, which included some significant partying, but they weren't ever pushing it on me. I could hang for a bit. When it was time to go, I would just go.

I was also playing better than I ever played before.

Still, three months into my recovery, I left Amen. I knew I had to put my recovery first. I said to myself, "Being in this band is the one thing that is causing me anxiety; it's fucking with my serenity." So I put in my notice. I finished the shows we had lined up, and I left, even though I didn't have another gig lined up. That was OK. I thought, "I've got to save my life." That was March 2002.

When I was eight months clean, I got a call from the drummer of the band Hed PE. I was old friends with those guys. We had toured the world together. They had opened for Snot. They asked me to join their band, but the offer was conditional. The first thing they asked me was, "Hey, Sonny, what's your party situation?"

I said, "I've been sober for eight months." They said, "Great. You want to join our band?" I did. I toured with those guys. I also started going to twelve step meetings on tour. That was an important part of my support and serenity. I could play clean, and I was the only one in the band who was clean at that time.

I played and toured with Hed until 2004. There was a lot of volatility in the band. Wes, who would become Rock to Recovery's founder, had already had a blowout with the singer and left the band he had founded right in the middle of a tour. The volatility in that band got to me too. When it came to writing new music and talking about moving forward, I did not have any interest in doing what the lead singer was doing. The new stuff was all about riding his skateboard to the liquor store high on meth. I'm not interested in that. That wasn't me anymore, so I left the band.

Although I went to work at a regular day job, I knew another music gig would develop. I got an audition for Nine Inch Nails. I had not been playing guitar at all since leaving Hed PE. I stuck to my twelve step program, but I fell back into some of that melancholy of my early life. Nine Inch Nails got me off my butt. I learned a bunch of their songs and then auditioned. I didn't get the gig, but I was playing again.

Then, sure enough, January 19 of '05, I got a call from Sevendust. The drummer asked, "Hey man, what's your party situation?" I said, "Bro, I've been sober for over three years." He said, "Cool. You want to join Sevendust?" I said, "Yes, I do." Literally eleven days later, I flew to Florida and recorded on what was the fifth Sevendust album, my first of three. It was great.

Every band has their dynamic of twisted relations, and Sevendust was no different from the others. But playing with them was fantastic. I was getting to live my dream. I was a worker for hire, but I was in all the photos. I wrote. I got insurance. I got a salary. It was the most professional situation I'd been in, and I loved playing music with those guys. It was so fun. The music was real high energy. It's kind of pissed off, but it's still fun.

That gig, too, came to an end, but this time it was a more

natural conclusion than I'd had in the past. The guy I replaced got sober and came back to Sevendust. Though he and I remained good friends, I was out of the band and out of a job.

Wesley, whom I'd played with when I was in Hed PE, had toured with Korn. He, too, was sober now, and when his time with Korn ended, he was already developing Rock to Recovery. When he mentioned the idea to me, I said, "Bro, I want in!" When he started doing his first sessions in June 2013, I immediately started to shadow him. I was so compelled to be part of it that I'd drive to Orange County, and he would buy me lunch, and I would spend the day down there. He didn't pay me. He couldn't. I didn't care. I wanted to be part of Rock to Recovery that much.

At lunch, we would talk and decide what was the best way to use what amp and how we could show people the simplicity and beauty of writing a song. We developed the methodology and the check-in questions and all of it. It was an incredible and inspiring time.

You know how we say, "You're rad"? That was something that just organically came out of me one day as we were doing check-ins. Somebody was hating on themselves for something, and I said, "Hey, you know what? You're rad." They were like, "Oh, thanks, man," and then everybody went, "Yeah!" The whole group went nuts, shaking shakers and making noise. Wesley looked at me with that "Oh, man, that worked!" expression. Then we did it for the next person and the next person. Now it's in the fuckin' training manual that you have to tell people that they're rad!

Eventually, the program expanded to treatment centers in LA, and Rock to Recovery became my full-time job. I've never had a job that has allowed me to be more genuinely myself than this one.

I am able to harness and use music to be creative, not to just play covers and stuff but to create with people who use what we empower them with to change their lives. I love to be able to empower people to make the music theirs. A friend of mine from Faith No More said of music, "Bro, we're playing with magic. We're making soil. We're making something to grow life from." And that's what music is: it's magic.

Sometimes, the music we create can be dark. When it is, I remember the Smokey Robinson song I liked so much and help the group go into those dark places. Clinicians don't always get it, but musicians understand that dark songs help people connect to and process dark feelings. You hear this in twelve step meetings too. People share their war stories, their darkest moments. Doing so helps us to connect to the blessings of recovery and the light we now experience. You can't feel the light if you haven't experienced the dark. Expressing and then illuminating the darkness in our lives has been one of the highlights of the songwriting process we engage in during our Rock to Recovery groups.

Rock to Recovery has improved my own recovery too. It has made me more tolerant, more patient, gentler, more understanding because I work so closely with the disease of addiction. We hear of people dying all the time, and sometimes it hits close to home. The morning I heard that our friend and colleague Christian had OD'd, I had literally just written a poem about reaching out to people who "wade in black tar." "I can reach for them and say, 'Let me help you,' but they can't always reach back." I wrote that poem because "just one more time" was on my mind. The single time that it's really only one more is the last time—and they're dead.

I called Wes as soon as I heard. An overdose death had never hit that close to home, especially in Rock to Recovery. We are all so close, and we didn't know that Christian was so far away. I guess we really never know. I can ask people, "Are you saying you're going to use? Let's talk about this." We can have enthusiasm and talk the talk, but there's always something underneath that has to be dealt with. Christian had stuff underneath that he just didn't give attention to and didn't show us.

I assume that people are doing well because I want them to be doing well. That doesn't make it so. We can only try. If anything, it is incredibly humbling. I'm feeling the vulnerability that is still in me as a recovered alcoholic/addict. If I don't continue to address my condition, I could be headed for trouble. I couldn't help Christian because I didn't know anything was wrong and because I'm not God. What I do have the power to do is reach toward something. The humility for me is in reaching for the solution every single day, no matter how long I am sober. I am so sad that there was nothing any of us could have done unless there had been something in him that said, "Help me."

Christian asked me to play "Running to Stand Still" by U2 with him at Wes' birthday party four weeks prior to his death. The magic of him asking me to play that song and then to play it with Constance at the memorial was a gift. Though I'd just had oral surgery the day before the memorial, I was determined to go. I wanted to play a song with Constance. She was singing and asked me to play the keyboard part. That also inspired me—that I got to play with Constance—because that song was so important and meant so much to her and to Christian. I was called to add my essence to the sum of the parts of the love for Christian and our Rock to Recovery fellowship. It keeps me close to my recovery—and when I say "my recovery," I'm referring to my daily life. Music and sobriety are not separate things. They are what I live and breathe and do.

I didn't get to help Christian, but I can help others. There was a guy I saw who just recently had relapsed. He had eight days. I had seen him for months at these two different places where I do sessions. He would bounce back and forth, and not once did he even shake a shaker. He would not participate in a session: "No, dude. I'm good. I'm good, bro. No." I let him be. I can't be responsible for anyone's recovery; I can only be a light.

For some reason, this past week, he sat behind the keyboard and played the damn bass line! He was fucking it up, but I said, "Buddy, don't worry about anything. When in doubt, just stop and look at me. I'll count you back in, and then you can start over. Don't worry about it. Just stay with me, man. It's OK. I got you." That's a life lesson that music teaches. You can start over. Stop. Breathe. And try again.

Eastern philosophy is also something I try to bring to the Rock to Recovery sessions. Since I was a kid, I was not into religion, but the principles of martial arts have been a guiding force throughout my life. My interest initially was just in the physical actions, though I don't practice anymore. I'm not violent; I do not want to hurt anyone. Specifically, for eastern wisdom, I appreciate Bruce Lee; I actually have a Bruce Lee tattoo. His thing was, "Be water."

This is an approach that I bring to Rock to Recovery. I don't walk in the room and say, "We are going to write a country song today." "We're gonna write a rockabilly song." "We're gonna write a metal song." Sometimes the band members go, "We don't know, Sonny. We don't really know." I say, "How about this?" and they say, "Yeah, let's do that." Sometimes I offer it up, but most of the time I say, "Hey, what style of music are you guys feeling?" They'll throw some stuff out, and then they'll say to each other, "Yeah, let's do that." I try to be like water and help them find the flow.

Bruce Lee said, "You put water in a cup, it becomes the cup. You put water into a bottle, it becomes the bottle. You put it in a teapot, it becomes the teapot." Water's one of the most powerful materials on the planet. It cuts into the earth. It cuts through stone eventually. It molds whole borders and coastlines. Water can crash, or it can flow. Sometimes we are mellow and flow. Sometimes we crash. Either way, there are lessons we can learn. Running water has a music all its own.

Be water, my friend.

3

BRANDON JORDAN

"Born of a Broken Man" by Rage Against the Machine

I am a second-generation LA native and a third-generation drug user. My father was a heroin addict. He tried to get clean and sober, but sobriety was hard for him. My parents separated when I was two, and my father OD'd a week after I turned four. He left treatment with a couple of other people. They went out to use "one more time." He overdosed in the back of a car, and the people he was with just dumped him onto a lawn where he died alone. Back then, you could go to jail for taking someone to the hospital who had OD'd, so he was not taken to a place that could help him. I've had similar experiences. I've woken up after being left for dead because I overdosed. I'm not here because I'm any braver or smarter or anything than my dad. I've just been given more chances than he had.

I only have one memory of my father. He was dope sick, lying on a beanbag chair. I asked, "Dad, what's the matter?" I was being a goofball, trying to entertain him, to get his attention. He said,

"Son, I'm so sick I can't even engage you right now." That's all I remember of him.

My drug of "choice" is heroin, just like his was. I put quotation marks around "choice" because I would have and did use anything I could get my hands on, but heroin was my preference. Once I found heroin, I said to myself, "I wanna do this every single day." I made similar choices to my father's later on in my life. I felt more like a man doing the same things as him. I wanted to have a similar life experience. Before I got clean and sober, the fact that I only had that one memory of him was really painful. But now that I'm clean and sober over ten years, I realize that I was spared a lot because my dad died young.

I knew at a young age there was something off with me. I wasn't sure what it was, but I had a sinking suspicion that whatever I'd do, I'd go all out. I wasn't just gonna be a stoner. I wasn't just gonna be a drinker. I'm drawn to the deep end. I'm dramatic, and I know it. I have always been a very intense person with a lot of energy and an anger problem. I was also terribly lonely growing up. We moved around a lot. My mom remarried a couple of times. By eleven or twelve, I was on my fourth father. Everything felt temporary to me. School. The dude my mom was with. Friends.

My way of dealing with the loneliness was to do everything full on. For instance, I was athletic, but by the time I was ten years old, I had broken my legs three times! The jock route to social connection was out. In fourth grade, I was such a nightmare on the playground that I wasn't allowed to go to recess. To prevent me from getting into a fight, I would be taken to the office. I didn't have recess. I didn't have lunch. I just went to the office and sat. Because I was far enough away from the other kids, the office staff would let me do laps around the office. They also let me listen to music. It was like 1988 or something. I had a Walkman, and this band Guns N' Roses had just put out an album called *Appetite for Destruction.* I listened to it constantly.

Like so many kids, my childhood dream was to make music. I grew up in the '80s. With my father gone, my mother was the breadwinner. She worked all the time to take care of the family. I spent many afternoons at family members' and their friends' houses. I was mostly around adults. One of the things I learned to do quickly to entertain myself was to take apart people's stereos and put in a microphone input. By using Scotch tape and a blank cassette, I could write and rap my own songs. I was drawn to the rhythm and the message of hip hop because it was the only music then that was talking about growing up in a fatherless home. I was also drawn to rock-and-roll. That's when I started writing lyrics for songs. I remember writing a song in fourth grade called "Live Like an Astronaut." I occupied myself in that office by writing songs. All afternoon, day after day, I made songs. It taught me to try to find the good in everything. If I hadn't been stuck in that office every day, I might not have become a songwriter.

What I had then was undiagnosed depression. I was a suicidal teenager who engaged in self-harm. I was abused by someone who lived with us, not related to me, but right there in the house. I tried to commit suicide twice. I wanted off the planet. A lot of my motivation to kill myself was revenge, to get back at the person who hurt me. I filled up the bathtub, then hit my head on the metal spigot to knock myself out and drown. I wanted that person to find me. It was a big "fuck you!" I wanted that person to have an "oh, shit!" moment. Looking back now, it was my attempt to manipulate and have some control over a situation in which I had no control. That was in my early teenage years. I might even have been only twelve. I battled with the depression but never sought help. I have never been good at asking for help. I needed people to believe I was a tough cookie who didn't need anybody's help, even in extreme and abusive situations. I was more concerned with what someone else thought of me than in getting support for the things that were happening to me. My real mistake is that I lived with the abuse and the self-hatred it created.

When I was twenty-one, I was out of the house on my own. I was financially secure. I had direction. I had just transitioned out of being in one band into a punk band we named KillRadio. I liked the deconstruction of punk rock. I liked art movements like surrealism and Dadaism that were smash-the-fucking-world-to-bits concepts because I don't like the world anyway. That's when I started using. That's late for most addicts. I was recreating that abusive behavior toward myself with drugs and alcohol. It felt right. When I abused myself, it felt normal. I started drinking. I started doing speed. Then I started smoking weed. For me, and I say this to a lot of the clients I work with, smoking weed was like I found the remote control on the negative voice in my head that is constantly judging me. Weed was the mute button, and that silence was awesome.

I got signed to a small record deal, which was sold to Columbia Records. I had gone from being this small-time, local dude to being signed with a major label. It happened really fast. My childhood dreams of playing and singing in a rock-and-roll band and writing songs came true. I got to travel the globe with my best friends, playing political punk rock music. I subverted the system to my benefit to have a corporation pay me to generate an anticorporate art message. The system paid me to do it. I worked really hard to make that happen and to be unique in my approach of how I did it. I upset people. I disrupted people. I loved it! I fought really hard to have a music career and yet try to disrupt any sort of normal path to having a career. This is what you do to have a punk rock career. We'd try to destroy ideas of some higher concept of what is punk rock. That's not what this book is about, but that's important to me, the ethos of the principles of what is punk rock.

As my recording and punk career got bigger, my drinking and using escalated as well. That's when I married a couple ideas together: I've had it worse than you, so I can get away with worse than you. I called it my "license to ill." I used that as a justification for not having to get better. I also used the fact that I was a musician as a justification for not having to get better, even though I knew that not all bands, all musicians, partied like I did. I came up with the band Rise Against, who were political and hard-hitting, and they were nice guys. I came up with another band called Anti-Flag. Onstage, it was f-bombs, but offstage it was highly intellectual. I saw the positive side of the rock-and-roll world, particularly punk rock, raising each other up and building a community. Real consciousness.

Though I saw the consciousness, I just wanted to get fucked up. I fell into the camp that said, "I see how I could be better, and it makes me feel worse because I can't reach those goals." I would wake up in the morning feeling like, "I want to be a good person, but I'm not gonna be able to because I'm going to medicate myself with this medicine that keeps making me a worse person."

My substance abuse took everything away from me. We had

representation that encouraged that behavior. I think any musical act has to have a quarterback; I was the quarterback for KillRadio, but my behavior was entirely self-destructive. The hardest thing for me was fighting to get to the major leagues, getting there, and losing it all. I was dropped by the record label, manager, and booking agent. I lost control of my team because I lost control of myself. People had to step in and take care of me. My friends in the band didn't respect me because I had no answers for them. The whole team was disassembled because there was no quarterback any longer.

I could not go seamlessly from, "I'm a punk rocker; fuck, we're gonna take over the world!" to needing to wait tables to pay the rent. The fall from grace was really hard for me. I felt like I had been the king of Los Angeles only to become homeless, living in a bush, and shooting drugs on the street.

I first sought help for my drug use after setting my manager's house on fire. I lit a candle and passed out. I woke up on fire on a couch that was burning. I put the fire out myself because I was so afraid, and I somehow made it out of there alive. That's when I asked for help. I had several members of Alcoholics Anonymous on both my parents' sides of the family with over thirty years sober. I called one of them and said I wanna go to a twelve step program.

I didn't get clean right off. I smoked weed at first, which led to the harder stuff coming back in. My first meeting was December 28, 2005, but I wasn't able to be clean and sober. I really became a thief at that point. My habit got way out of control. I had probably a hundred-dollar-a-day habit, which is a lot of heroin. I stole anything I could and pawned it.

One of my family members stepped in and said, "You might

need a medical detox." I went to rehab in 2006. I went back to the twelve step program and worked the steps. I went to sober living. I worked through MAP, the Musicians' Assistance Program. I stayed clean for nine months, but in the back of my mind, I thought maybe I could smoke weed.

One of my lowest points was coming out of a job interview in a crumpled suit and tie a couple months into sobriety. I saw a fan of the band wearing our t-shirt. I said, "What's up? Thanks for the support"

He said, "You're not in that band. Look at you. Why are you in a suit and tie?" I had to take off the jacket and the collared shirt and say, "Look at this," pointing to the tattoo on my forearm. "Who else has this tattoo?"

He said, "No shit. You are coming out of a California Pizza Kitchen, you fucking loser." All my fears were realized. I said to myself, "It's over." I had lost my punk rock card. I wanted a way out. I found a joint on the ground and thought it was a gift from God. I did think for a moment that I might call my sponsor, but I went with "gift from God" because I'm so spiritual. Within forty-five minutes, I was in the 'hood looking for more stuff. I found out that the thing I have to check at the door if I wanna get stoned is sober mentality and clarity. I don't get to bring that into stoned land. Once I was stoned, it was much easier to say, "Fuck it." That was March 2007. Within three days of smoking that first joint, I overdosed. Then I went at it hard.

My bottom was living in a house with men who were prostitutes, tricking themselves out to pay for their fixes. They were straight guys who had to do homosexual acts to supply their habit. I was new to the scene, but I was learning their ways. Literally, I was walking down the street trying to put a price tag on what I would be worth when I had a real moment of clarity. I said, "This is not your mom's fault. It's not the fact that your dad died. It's not the fact that your music career didn't work out. It's nobody else's deal other than yours. You are the only reason why you're walking down the street trying to put a price tag on your body." I got back into recovery. My sobriety date is October 15, 2007.

I got into a detox through Tarzana Treatment Center. I had been at their needle exchanges so often I was on a first-name basis with the people there. I was in really bad shape. They asked if I'd like some help and thought that maybe they could get me a county bed. I took them up on it. I was there for two or three weeks.

After that, I went to an LA County-run facility for four months. It wasn't just a rehab. It was out in the woods with barbed wire and three hundred other people, some homeless and some men getting out of prison after more than a decade. There were gangs and a lot of racial shit. It was pretty fucking gnarly. The security guards were selling speed. Guys were getting Purell sent to them through the mail and using electric toothbrushes to heat it up so the alcohol would come to the top. They would spoon it out and get lit like no one's business.

I stayed sober. I wanted it.

I put music away. My first sobriety I had been very resentful at all the people who had come up with us, or maybe even opened up for us, and were now famous. When you're sitting in treatment and you're listening to the radio and the opening bands for your band are now blowing up on the radio and you're sitting in rehab, I was resentful at not having made it. I was resentful that I couldn't tell the story to family members, or the world, or the people who hurt me: "Fuck you. I made it."

When I got sober that second time, I wasn't going to let any music career define me. I just let the sobriety date define me, threw myself into being sober and not worrying about my old music, my old band, anything like that. I let it go. I didn't think I'd ever play music again. I was OK with that.

If I picked up a guitar, if I sang something, it was just for me. I had no ambition outside self-soothing. I was also afraid of playing music because I played really loud, angry music. I didn't know how to transition to a place where I was playing music just for fun.

Fun wasn't what I had been doing with music. My music was a vehicle for a message. To just get down to the purity of a guitar sounding good was hard. It didn't have to be a tool to kill fascists. Slowly, I learned to play and sing because a guitar sounds good, and so does my voice. I came to think that's why you should play and sing.

I became a facilitator with Rock to Recovery through my sponsor. It's very different work from being in a band. There is a lot that's different in good ways, and there's a lot that's just different. One of the best things about Rock to Recovery is we write and play a song at the same time. Then we record it. Everything has a clock on it.

The challenge is to write the first draft. It is my job to invite people to the idea that we can't judge ourselves and create at the same time. I only want them to wear one hat. I always joke with the participants. I'll say, "Did you hear me invite Judge Judy to this party?" When they say no, I say, "Then stop judging yourself and just get into the music."

People who participate in a Rock to Recovery session think that what we do is some sort of miracle. They think it is a miracle that we write a song in an hour and a greater miracle when the song is pretty good. The miracle is not that the song is good. The miracle is that people drop the cloak that they have to be perfect. The miracle is that people stop thinking they can't do something.

We're there to push them in the right direction. Sometimes it lines up where the right person is in the right mentality to write an uplifting song, and they are connected. They just drop the cloak of "I have to be any sort of way other than here in the moment." The song gets written. The miracle is that they're not thinking about outside stresses: being a mother, a drug addict, saddled with debt, facing a drug charge. I've had sessions with a guy who had just committed vehicular manslaughter; he killed two people going the wrong way on the freeway. The miracle is not that we wrote a song that's awesome; the miracle is that he was only concerned about the next note and what he could give, not about the fact that he might spend the next five years in prison.

When I was in treatment, people told me all the time, "Be in the now. Be present. Don't be in the future or the past." That's one of the problems with recovery. People speak in clichés. They give all this advice that has no instructions. You can wake up in the morning in treatment with advice fatigue. Who's gonna tell me that I'm screwing up my life today? It pissed me off when I was in treatment that they would give me advice without telling me how to follow it. Telling people to be in the now is great advice that has no instructions. In Rock to Recovery, we give people the instructions. We don't talk about playing music. We play music.

The instructions are like, "This is the first note. I want you to play it four times. This is the second note. I want you to play it four times. The third note, I want you to play two times. After you play the third note, go back to one. Back at one, you're going to circle all over again. It's gonna be a cycle. We'll call that our verse. I'm going to write those numbers in purple.

"Now I'm gonna write a couple more numbers in green. That's gonna be the chorus. The chorus is where we make our money. What's the color of money? Green. When you see green, I want you to think chorus. I want that to be the first note. You're gonna go to the green number one; then you're gonna go to number two. You're gonna cycle back and forth because music is like a merry-go-round. It's like a monopoly board; when you get to the end, you're right at the beginning."

Watching this process reminds me that it all comes back to the constant that there's a power greater than me that I can always reach out to. That's what being a facilitator with Rock to Recovery does for me. It reminds me that there's a Higher Power, and, in that moment, music can be the Higher Power. It inspires me to make that available to others.

Sometimes they get it; sometimes they don't. In 2018, I worked with twelve people who died, and I just found out about them; it could be more. When you work in treatment, you often only get news when it's bad. When I hear someone say, "Did you hear about…?" I assume an overdose. I did sessions at a treatment center where we had three people die within six weeks. They were in the sessions with each other, and they loved it. And Christian, who OD'd, was one of us. I take it personally. The closer I am to the person, the more personally I take it. I'm still not over Christian. His death shows me how much work I still have to do.

When people overdose—and even with Christian—when my clients die, it initially brings up the old wound of my dad dying. My reaction is anger: fuck you for making me think of my dead dad, who I really don't remember. But now I can take that energy and transform it into gratitude, and that keeps me going: Thank you for reminding me who I can be. I am not my father. I don't want anyone to have the "Did you hear about" conversation about me, and they could.

At the end of the day, I keep doing the work because it's the right thing to do. We're in Rock to Recovery for the purity of doing the right thing. We might save some lives, and we might not. And we might do something to help change the world.

Shattered Dagger

By Mike

Forged by fire with a razor's edge,
born for war, loyalty is pledged,
mirrored, finished with a golden hilt,
broken by battle, bloodied, scarred with
guilt.

(chorus)
Darkness attacks me from within;
This time the battle is mine to win;
Refuse to back down to the dark,
Dagger's bite worse than the bark.
All I have is in this fight,
Armed myself with the light;
Claw my way out of this hell,
Myself to save for those who fell.

Brothers and sisters lost to war,
not sure what it means anymore;
save each other from the ground,
only then redemption found.

Dagger's used now every day
just to keep the dark away.
Fight this war to save each other,
Fight for my sisters and brothers.

(chorus)
Darkness attacks me from within;
This time the battle is mine to win.
Refuse to back down to the dark,
Dagger's bite worse than the bark.
All I have is in this fight,
Armed myself with the light;
Claw my way out of this hell,
Myself to save for those who fell.

Mike's story appears later in this book.

4

PHIL BOGARD

"Behind My Guitar" by Ingram Hill

The first time I got drunk enough to throw up, I was in the seventh grade. I drank a whole six-pack of beer and threw it up all over my best friend's floor. Beer was just the worst-tasting thing ever. Pot was better, but in that part of the South, between Nashville and Memphis, it was a bunch easier to get my hands on beer.

I'd been experimenting with drugs for a while before that. I was maybe ten years old the first time I smoked a cigarette. Cigarettes were my gateway drug, like it was for the rest of my generation. But once I got to the seventh grade, I smoked pot and ate acid and tried cocaine. None of that really stuck. But liquor, that was my drug. Lots of musicians drank, and I was going to be a musician. On an epic level.

I'd been playing guitar since I was eight years old. When my dad's friends came over to the house, he wasn't one of those "show the guys your fast ball" dads. He'd be like, "Play that Beatles song you just learned." I never even thought about another career.

We'd always assumed I'd go to college, and I wanted to go as a music major with a specialty in guitar. If you wanted to do that, you had to audition. The very first college I auditioned for was Temple University in Philadelphia. I flew up there with all these pieces of music I'd composed. I mean I'd written string quartets, brass quartets, all kinds of stuff. I had all the classical pieces I played, and I'd practiced until I was perfect. I was really ready.

I was one of the last auditions of the day, and the professor asks me my name. When I answer, I call him "sir." And he says, "Sir? Are you from the South?" I say, "Yes, sir." And he says, "Oh, God. Let's get this over with."

Right away, I'm much more nervous than I had been. I pick up my guitar to play a piece called "Prelude No. 4," and I slide into the first note. He drops his notebook and starts laughing, so I stop playing. He asks, "Why'd you do that? Who taught you that? Is that the way they play in *the South*?" I'm so thrown by that that my hands start to shake. And you can't play guitar if your hands are shaking uncontrollably. Do I need to say I didn't end up going to Temple? Or any other place in the North? I went back to the South and enrolled in Landon University in Jackson, Tennessee.

Music majors at Landon have to play in front of all the heads of the music department. One of those folks was a lady who got off on making students feel small, and her sarcasm caused me to have an instant flashback to the guy at Temple. My hands immediately started shaking again. I could play when it was fun, no problem. Hanging out with my buddies, playing in front of folks on campus or even in bars, that was OK. But turn on bright lights and hook up amps, tell me that it was important, that it was a paying gig, that kind of circumstance, put me onstage opening for Edwin McCain, and the shaky hands came roaring back.

I wanted to be in a band. I didn't want to shake. And what I figured out made my hands steady was a couple of beers. Drink the beers, and it was like the road smoothed out, and I became Keith Richards. It would've been great, but the thing was that a couple of beers became a bunch of beers, a six-pack, and then a twelve-pack. But we were a good band, and we were on our way. That band became Ingram Hill. We started getting college radio play, did a bunch of frat parties. Our first year, we did 181 shows, and of course I was drinking for most of them.

In our second year, I remember we were doing the kind of party where I wouldn't have to do a lot of beer, but I hit a sour note, and it freaked me out. Probably nobody was aware of it but me, but the moment I heard myself do it, my hands started shaking. I about ran to the beer keg they had at the party and chugged three big cups. I think that was when it started to be, "If I'm playing a guitar in front of anybody at all, I have to drink to do it. And I have to drink enough to be sure." That was in 2001.

In 2003, we signed with a big label. That was like the dream of my childhood was coming true. The rest of the guys felt the same. That's what we wanted, making good music that people listened to and loved. There was even a moment in time when we were one of the best bands out there, firing on all cylinders. For me, the alcohol I was drinking was like my fuel, my guarantee that I'd play my best. It really worked. It got me onstage with steady hands, and it made my performances work. I might make a fool of myself offstage and do things I'd regret later; I might have shaky hands every day after a while until I piled on the alcohol, but onstage, I was gold.

By the time I was twenty-two, I was drinking a minimum of

twelve beers a day, along with a couple of big bottles of vodka as a
kicker. If I only drank beer, it was probably close to thirty or forty
a day.

When the label decided we'd peaked and dropped us, my
drinking was out of control. It wasn't just to get onstage anymore. I
drank to get up in the morning, to get dressed, to take out the trash.
And I got to be paranoid about people finding out how much I was
really drinking, so I never put my bottles in the trashcan. I didn't
want the neighbors to see. I had this walk-in closet, and it got filled
with beer bottles, vodka bottles. I knew it wasn't good, but I had
to do it.

If I went a few hours without drinking, like when I slept at
night, I'd go into a kind of instant withdrawal, which I didn't even
recognize. I just knew that I'd wake up shaking and that I couldn't
digest food properly. I was always throwing up. It's like I was unin-
tentionally bulimic. I'd eat something, and it would just come back
up, and I'd go on throwing up until all that came out was bile.

I'd wake up shaking, and the only way I could stop shaking and
stop throwing up was to drink even more. But through that time, I
kept playing with the band.

We had been booked to play a Minneapolis Colts Fan Appreciation event. We set out to drive there in our van, which is how
we got to gigs at that time. The day we left, I drank a twelve-pack
of beer for breakfast, and then we stopped at a gas station and
got more beer, and I drank that, but beer makes you pee, and we
couldn't keep stopping, so I figured I'd wait until dinner and drink
a bunch then, when they had a restroom handy. Only we ended
up stopping at a Cracker Barrel, and they don't sell booze there. I

ate dinner then went to the bathroom and threw it all up. Standard procedure for me.

We got back on the road again, but all of a sudden, I started having audio hallucinations. It sounded like the guys' voices were whipping around in my head, and then my entire body started shaking, not just my hands, and I blacked out.

When I came to, we were on the side of a road, and a police officer was shining a light in my face and saying, "Phil! Can you sit up? I need you to talk to me." I got up, and the officer starts asking me questions I should have known how to answer, but for some reason, I can't think of answers, just excuses about why I'm not answering. "Do you know what day it is?" "I'm a musician. We don't need to know what day it is." "Do you know what state you're in?" "We're traveling." The officer says, "We're gonna get an ambulance to take you to a hospital." And I'm like, "I don't have health insurance, and I'm not going to spend the rest of my life paying off an ambulance ride." I would only go to the hospital if they didn't call an ambulance.

At the hospital ER, they ultimately diagnosed me with DTs, delirium tremens, and it turned out that I had not just passed out; I had had a grand mal seizure. I know now that only about 10 percent of alcoholics drink to the point of delirium tremens, and of those people, of which I was clearly one, about 80 percent will die during one of the seizures. When I learned that, it was a real game changer for me but not in a good way. It made me certain that I couldn't stop drinking or I'd die. I switched over from beer to vodka and Gatorade. I'd been scared out of my skin by that seizure, and I was living in perpetual fear of it happening again.

My routine to stave off ever having to feel again like I did on the road was to wake up in the morning and drink until I passed out. And when I woke up again later in the day, I did it again. There were times when I didn't know if it was day or night. I did that for three months. There were no good moments. The buzz I used to get, that feeling of being Keith Richards, any ambition I had, they were all gone.

Then one day, one of my bandmates, Justin, came over and handed me a CD of our last performance together, and I'm thinking, "Here comes an intervention. He's going to tell me I screwed up the band. And then he'll leave, and I can make myself another drink." But Justin didn't say anything about the band. He said, "The hell with you. You're killing me watching you doing this to yourself! I've known you since we were kids, and you're my brother, and you think it's OK with me that you're going to kill yourself, and I have to watch you die? How would you feel if I put a gun in my mouth and blew my brains out in front of you? What would I be saying to you by doing that? I love you, man, and I have to say fuck you for putting me in this position."

That was the magic moment. That was when the universe aligned for me. I suddenly got it, that I'd been lying to myself all along, that I had told myself I was only doing this to me. At that moment, I thought about my parents and how they would feel to see me die. And it was like, "Holy shit, I'm doing this to them. I'm making them suffer." I went into rehab in August 2008.

I had a long, very rough detox. I had people who were coming off heroin looking at me in the rehab and going, "God almighty, what were you on? Why do you look so bad?" Well, coming off alcohol at the level I was on was like having poison in every cell of my body. They had to load me up on drugs in rehab, Ativan and Valium, to keep me from seizing and maybe dying. They monitored me because they couldn't get my blood pressure down, and they were afraid I'd stroke out. When I left the rehab, I was on three blood pressure meds. I was twenty-eight and at the top of the class for liver damage. But when you're as young as I was, the liver can heal, and mine mostly did.

I left rehab sober. I went back to Ingram Hill, and it was like coming home. I wrote songs for the band, and I found out that on the front end of sobriety we get a lot of grace. When I was sixty days sober, we went on tour, and I was playing, and the shaky hands didn't show up, but whatever had caused them came crashing in as a fear of getting dizzy and fainting in front of an audience. We were playing festivals and theater shows, and I'm starting to hate myself for being weak and not in any kind of control.

I called a guy who'd been kind of a spiritual mentor to me all my career, and who also went through recovery, and I told him how I was shaky inside this time. He said, "Look, that's how you feel, and the harder you fight it, the more you'll feel it. Just ride it." I tried. I was determined I wasn't going to go back to drinking. I was miserable.

Then we were playing a theater show with a band called the Clarks, based out of Pittsburgh, who were really hot in the Northeast. Ingram Hill had done our gig, and I'm standing backstage talking to the guys from that band, and one of them chugs a Corona. I remember what it felt like back when drinking a beer was a good experience for me, and I could feel that memory in my whole body. I ran outside and called a guy who was kind of like a sponsor. When I told him what just happened, he said, "Hey, that's great news." I'm like, "What?" He said, "We know you're an alcoholic, and we know the solution to alcoholism. You walked away. Good work."

That was the start of my climb out. The fear still came back in waves, but they got shallower and shallower. Finally, they might still come, but they have less and less power over me. The gigs got bigger. We opened for Lynyrd Skynyrd with thirty thousand in the crowd, and I played it stone-cold sober.

In 2013, Ingram Hill broke up, and I moved to Nashville, where I ended up with Jelly Roll playing hip hop for the drug culture. We were mega-successful, touring, and I did lots of gigs stone-cold sober. Sometimes I think I was the only sober one among, like, twenty thousand people, and that's a trip in itself. Then I got an offer to go with Walker McGuire, and I went. It was taking gigs all over the country. It was wonderful to be doing that, like a dream come true, for a while.

Something changed when we landed in San Diego for five days. We only had to do one show and some publicity, and for the rest of the time we just hung out. I started feeling like I'd been going full speed for a long time, like twenty years, and I just wanted to hold still, be in the moment. I felt like I was ready for something different, and maybe I could not just stay in a good place but help other people too.

Who were the people that I really wanted to help? People who were in the trap I'd been in before I got sober. So I went to the corporate offices for a treatment center with a bunch of facilities across the country. I don't always know what I'm doing, but I kind of trust the universe to guide me. I really didn't have any intention of applying for a job with that company; I was just curious. But I feel like if I have good intentions, and I trust my gut, there'll be something good happening.

What happened was that they told me about Rock to Recovery, run by a guy from Korn. I didn't know if it was something you volunteer for or what. I thought I might sometime check it out.

Now, I've had a long-term, good relationship with MusiCares, which is the charitable arm of the GRAMMYs. One of the things they do is send musicians who don't have health insurance to get treatment. So I made contact with a friend there and asked, "If I wanted to do something like what you're doing, what kind of background do I need? Should I have a degree in something? And do you know anything about an organization by that guy from Korn?"

My friend asked, "Are you talking about Rock to Recovery? I'm on the board of directors for it." Pretty soon, I was on the phone with Wes, and that was another magical moment in my life. It felt so meant to be that it was impossible to do anything except get involved.

Back when I was first in recovery, they told me that musicians and artists and the like were the people most likely to be successful in rehab because they could take their experiences and confront them through their work. I was lucky to have the music part because music has a magic of its own. Literally. Singing fires off both halves of the brain and releases all the good chemicals, the oxytocin, the serotonin, the dopamine. It gives you a natural high, and I'd seen that it ultimately worked great for me. Working with the people who walk into the room where a session is going on is like a spiritual blast for me. I connect with them, and I feel like I am really alive in the world. A lot of them connect with me because I was Jelly Roll's guitarist, and I've played on some of the songs they listen to when they're in dark places.

Making that connection beats playing a gig in front of thousands of people. Hearing somebody tell me, "Dude, thank you. I was ready to walk out of here today, and I don't know what you did, but I feel good now" makes me feel I'm in the right place doing the right stuff. I mean how good is it to watch someone change right in front of your eyes and to know you helped that happen?

Sometimes things don't work out. I've seen friends I thought were going to make it fall back into the trap. Even close friends like another Rock to Recovery musician, Christian. Christian OD'd, and that was like a gut punch. The little bit of time I spent with him made me feel extra-close to him, and we're like a family in this company. We lost one of our own. But we couldn't make his decisions for him any more than anybody could make my decisions for me. He didn't come through the darkness. I am thankful I did.

5

BRANDON PARKHURST

"Know Good" by Yovee

My addiction story started with candy when I was a young kid. My dad came home one day and got a call from the school principal. The principal told him that he had walked around the corner to find a line of kids standing outside the bathroom. As he walked inside the bathroom past all the kids, I was standing in the front of the line trading clippings of *Playboy* that I had stolen from my dad for candy. I was hustling in the third grade. I was feeling good; I liked it. My dad couldn't even get pissed at me. He was like, "Man, he's a hustler." I started young.

I smoked weed not long after the candy hustle. I was walking to the bus stop one day with a couple buddies. I think I was twelve years old. I looked down in the gutter, and I saw a joint there. I knew what a joint was; I used to get *Mad Magazine*. I said, "That's a joint." We grabbed it and put it in my backpack. At school, we devised a plan to smoke the joint later. When school got out, we went to the liquor store. We invented this thing we called "Hey duding it." It's like, "Hey, dude, can ya buy me a six-pack of beer?" So we got a six-pack of beer.

There were three of us. We went to our skateboard ditch. I drank two beers, and I took two hits of that joint. When that kicked in, I was running around going, "Are you guys feeling this right now?" At that point, I was peeling an orange for forty-five minutes straight. It was like this slow-motion movie. I'm peeling the orange; it was spraying all over. I ate it. I was going, "You guys, this is the day!" I still get chills when I talk about that day.

Here's the catch about that whole thing. After that, I went home and went to bed. When I woke up in the morning, guess what? Nothing bad happened. I wasn't in trouble. No one knew. It was fine. That's the thing. People don't talk about it enough in recovery. Why wouldn't I eventually turn into a drug addict? When I started, I had a great freakin' time. I didn't get in trouble. The consequences weren't there.

After that day, my life was fun for a while. It was like girls, weed, beer, a little bit of coke, whatever, party, go to the beach. When I showed up places, people were like, "Brandon's here!" Fast-forward twenty-four more years: when I showed up somewhere, people were like, "Ugh, that guy's here." It was not that way in the beginning.

After that first doobie, my gettin' loaded train freakin' just took off.

In high school, I was always smoking weed before class. I think I had two periods of surf PE. I think I was in one class, and then I was a teacher's assistant in surf PE. I had this perfect little bong spot in my truck. "Red-Eye Express" is what the teachers called me when I walked in for regular classes after surfing. "Red-Eye Express is here." I was like, "OK." I mean I tried to play it off, but I knew deep down inside they were onto the fact that I was stoned out of my mind.

My relationships started to fall apart. I was lying to my parents. I started not showing up to school. From here, I can start to see it switch. I started sniffing coke; that's when I crossed this invisible line. What happened was I started getting consequences. That's the big shift, right about the time I got out of high school. I started lying, cheating. I couldn't show up anymore. If I did show up, I was gonna get my bag of weed or drink or whatever first.

A normal person, when they start getting consequences for drinking and using, says two words: I quit. I knew that was true because I had friends who I was smoking and drinking and getting into a little bit of coke with, but when the consequences hit, they were able to peel off and go, like, "I'm done." That didn't even cross my mind.

What crossed my mind was, "I'll switch it up. I'll manage it. I won't drink hard liquor anymore. I'll just drink beer. Or I'll only smoke weed. I'll only drink red wine. I'll only drink on Friday and Saturday. I'll only get one gram every third Friday of the month," like trying to manage it all. My new plan worked for a little bit of time, but, inevitably, it got worse.

By this point, I was nineteen. I was best buddies with this guy Adrian. I was having fun drinking, using, ignoring a little bit of con-sequences. Adrian came over. He was a surfer and a musician. He was two years older than me. He just looked cool. A girl would walk in the room and lock onto him because he was so good-looking. And he says, "You have to check this stuff out." He had heroin.

We had no idea really what we were doing. Nowadays, kids

are doing heroin instead of weed, but back then, we didn't know. I
wasn't scared at all. I went right to the needle. It's a miracle that I
made it through. But, anyway, I shot up and nodded out.

When I woke up, Adrian was blue. I ran out. I didn't know what
had happened. I didn't say anything to anybody. I just went home.
I figured he'd come to and be fine, that this is just what happens.

Two days later, I was at a friend's house. I wasn't even thinking
about Adrian; I was going on with my life. Anyway, at this friend's
house, we were all drinking and partying. Back then, we had land-
lines, and the landline rang. My friend answered the phone. She
listened for a second and then threw the receiver down. It hit me.
"Oh, Adrian. He's dead." She freaked out. I ran. I said, "I'm not gonna do that shit anymore. I'm not gonna do heroin anymore. I'll just
drink and smoke weed," which I stuck to until my next friend died
right in front of me later on. There's been a lot of that in my life,
but Adrian was the first. I had so much shame and guilt because
of Adrian's death. At the funeral, I didn't say anything. I was pet-
rified. I wondered if I could have saved him even though he was
dead when I came to and left the house. It was a heavy weight for a
nineteen-year-old.

The compulsion to use, though, it's hard to overcome. I said
I didn't want to use, but I didn't always have control. I could be
sitting at a red light going, "I'm not gonna get loaded today. I never wanna get loaded again. I'm gonna go surfing. I'm hanging out
with someone positive. I've got some days clean." The light would
turn green. I would start driving. About four stoplights on, my car
would go on autopilot and make a left turn. I'd go, "I don't wanna
go left. I'm supposed to be going straight to the beach." But there
I was, on my way to get loaded. How long does it take to go four

stoplights—like a minute? I started to understand during that time that it didn't matter how much I wanted to be clean. I could wanna be clean all I want, but something deeper inside me was navigating. Once I start, I can't stop. If I muster up all of my will and get all kinds of support, maybe I can stop for a little while, but I can't stay stopped. That's the thing. I can't stay stopped. And that's the problem with this whole addiction and alcoholism piece. Even when I'm not using, I'm still a prisoner.

Some of my friends didn't make it.

I had this condo in Encinitas where I lived. My friend was using heroin in this house, though I decided not to for years, since Adrian died. I think I was twenty-seven. We were up all night drinking. Everyone else had left. He came in the room from outside on the patio. He had a panicked look as he walked past me. He went into the bedroom and pulled an AK-47 out of his closet. He sat down against the wall with the gun up against his chest and pulled the trigger. Bam! I looked over. He had shot himself. He died in my arms. His name was Jimmy. He was gonna be a good skateboarder. Like that's not crazy enough, here's the really crazy part. The ambulance came. The police officers came. I knew one police officer; he played guitar. He said, "Brandon, what are you doing? This is getting bad." They took Jimmy out. Jimmy was gone. He was dead. They'd taken him out. The cops were there. There was blood all over the place, and the first thing I did when the cops left was go through Jimmy's stuff and get his heroin.

That started my bottom. Even after I wanted to stop, it took me six years to get sober.

But before all that, I went on tour, the biggest tour of my career. My band, Kut U Up, had been asked to go on this tour a year prior with Green Day, Blink 182, and Jimmy Eat World. It was the golden ticket for any young band. "We wanna take you guys on tour, give you a bunch of money. You drink and smoke a ton of weed and make a movie out of it." Who could say no?

The movie, *Riding in Vans with Boys,* was on MTV. We were an OK band, but we were taking off. Literally, when we got off of the tour, DreamWorks, the movie company, was gonna put out a record. Kut U Up was about to hit! We had a record deal. We came home from this huge tour. The world was opening up for us, and I was coming right off of that when Jimmy died, and I went back on heroin. I couldn't hang.

We had a manager who kept saying, "If you can just write eight songs, they don't even have to be good; just write them." I couldn't do it. I couldn't be present. For three years after my friend shot himself and I got back into heroin, I remember small glimpses of people kinda sitting me down saying, "We gotta write these songs." I literally thought it had been a month, but it was three years. I came out of this, like, three-year blackout. Of course, by that point, the opportunities were gone.

It went like that until I was thirty-one years old. When I came to, no one was around anymore.

After my three-year downhill spiral and not really knowin' about what recovery was, I decided to get clean. I had no idea how difficult that would be.

I went to my first detox. It was a seven-day detox. They call it "spin dry." They dried you out, and off you went. I went in. I got seven days clean. On the seventh day, I was a new man. I'll never forget that I was upstairs in the detox, making my bed, folding my clothes. I was whistling. It was day seven, and I was about ready to leave. I was clean. Nothing could go wrong, right?

As I went to leave, this woman from the detox center said, "We talked to your family, and we talked to the clinical staff. We suggest you stay here for twenty-eight days." My jaw hit the ground. Now I had just told someone in the detox that I would do anything to stay clean and have this new life. But what came out of my mouth was, "Twenty-eight days! I have seven days clean. Did they not tell you or something?" I continued, saying about fifteen "evers." "I will never, ever, ever, ever, ever...use drugs or alcohol again in any capacity for the rest of my life." And I believed it.

I went home that day, and by the morning, I was completely loaded. If you had given me a lie detector test in that detox, I would've passed it saying I never wanted to get loaded again. It took me less than twenty-four hours to be back in the vicious cycle of detox, inpatient, intensive outpatient program (IOP), sober living, relapse, detox, inpatient, IOP, sober living, relapse. That's the life until you get sober or die.

What happened for me, years later, was that I rolled into a twelve step meeting. I weighed 135 pounds. I looked like a skeleton. My eyes were sunk back in my head and yellow. I had jaundiced skin. My skin had that kinda pasty, sweaty, like constantly kinda wet feel. I was about to die. At that meeting, a guy came up to me and said, "Hey, man, you need to get honest about your drinking and using. You say you're an alcoholic and an addict, but do you know what that means?"

All of a sudden, the stars aligned. I realized I had no idea what it meant to have this problem. I realized that I was just a visitor to recovery. Then he said, "Well, let me tell you something. You have a brain that at some point in the future is gonna convince you that it's a good idea to get loaded again, for sure. It's not if; it's when. The day is coming, two minutes, two years; it doesn't matter. As soon as that thought comes, you're going to get loaded unless you learn what it means to be an alcoholic."

He was saying, "You're f'd. You're screwed." I was like, "This guy is right." Something came over me.

The biggest thing that's happened in my recovery is I was always a "no" guy. I'd come into recovery, and, literally, people would come up to me and be like, "Man, I've got twenty years clean. If you do this, this, this, and this, you'll have twenty years clean too." And I'd say, "OK, cool. I'll do the first thing you said, but I'm definitely not doing those other things." I always had resistance. "It's good for you guys, but I don't need that."

I think there is a word that we're probably not too familiar with in our early recovery. The word is "humility." What humility means is that I'm willing to admit that I don't know how to do it, and someone else might. It's a simple premise, but I almost died before I learned it. I knew a lot of guys, like Adrian and Jimmy, who never got there. I learned a lot of important lessons like, "Man, stick around here long enough to see what happens to people who don't stick around." I also learned, "If you feel like drinking or using today, it's not that you wanna drink or use; it's that you don't wanna feel how you're feeling." I had never understood that before, but I knew it was right. I didn't wanna feel anything. You die; I'm gonna get loaded. You get married; I'm gonna get loaded. Chargers win; I'm gonna get loaded. Chargers lose; I'm gonna get loaded. It doesn't matter. It's any feeling.

After I gave up and decided that I couldn't get loaded anymore, I started to work on spirituality. I knew that I was beyond human aid because that's what all the humans were telling me. Not one person could keep me sober. And if no human could keep me sober, I needed to look someplace else. I engaged with meditation and therapy, and I learned how to show up for myself. For me, the process of recovery was mainly about putting myself in connection with something greater than myself that could help me solve my problems, and that's what happened. My life started to change. I got a job at a treatment center and then, later, with Rock to Recovery. I recognized that my life is a spiritual journey.

I started to grow up. That's the biggest blessing that's happened to me. I've been able to turn into a man through the process of recovery and spiritual development. It's what I've always wanted. I reached out, and the world of recovery, including Rock to Recovery, reached in and pulled me off the death spiral. I get to be in this world and participate fully in life because of the love and support of the people around me.

I share the power of recovery through Rock to Recovery. Not only do I love the work that I do, but I get paid for holding my guitar and staying sober. I know I am blessed. I could have never thought up an opportunity like Rock to Recovery when I got clean. If someone had said to me when I was kicking dope, "Dude, this professional musician is going to pay you a good amount of money to play music with people in recovery," I would not have believed it. I took a risk and made a decision to get clean. I got vulnerable, and the world showed up for me.

I have been with Rock to Recovery since the beginning. I got to watch the whole thing grow. I also get to see how I have grown.

I notice the difference in myself, and so does everybody else. I am a completely different human being because of Rock to Recovery. It's a beautiful thing.

I want to be clear about something. I do Rock to Recovery because I like it. I like the feeling of bringing music to people. I get to help people, and I feel good about myself because of it. Anyone else can have this same feeling. You can do whatever you want if you take the risk of having a new experience of yourself. If you put in the work, show up, and not run from your fears, you can have the life you want too.

I'm also a Core Energetics practitioner. In this practice, we help deeply wounded people process traumas stored in the body. I get to walk them through the process of feeling their feelings and letting them out. I'm an assistant teacher at the school where I learned this process. I feel connected to something way more powerful than drugs or alcohol. My life is not perfect, but I can live an imperfect life and be grateful for it.

I've had five really close friends die from OD or suicide. I'm somewhat desensitized to it. It's sad. It's painful. But I get it because I know that pain, the desire to give up. The most recent was Christian Heldman. He was a Rock to Recovery program administrator like me. He was also my roommate and a close friend. Christian didn't decide to die; he made the decision to get loaded. I understand that decision.

It makes me scared. It shows me how easily that could be me. Shit. This is serious stuff. I know how to make the pain go away. I've got money to get it. I know how to cook it. I'm a hustler. I don't not do drugs and alcohol because they're hard to get. One bad decision is all it takes. And it happens fast. I felt Christian was having a problem on a Friday. By the following Tuesday, he was dead. Adrian. Jimmy. Christian. People I've worked with in treatment facilities. So many die. I always think, "Who's next?" It makes me want to do my work and be a resource and have people around me know that I'm not going to judge them. I want to be the person in people's lives who isn't going to judge.

If I take responsibility and get the support I need, I can walk through any fear and realize that it will not kill me. As I continue to walk through these fears, they become less and less controlling. I'm not dominated by my old blocks, negative emotions, and past traumas. I got out before death got me.

Everything I always wanted was right on the other side of my fears. Now I have a new experience of myself, the one I was looking for with drugs and alcohol but couldn't get to. I have a new life because I have support. I get to bring my whole self out to the world and have an impact on others and myself.

There's one more thing I really wanna say. This is important to me. Recovery has given me a car. I have a killer house. I have some money. I've got a bunch of friends. I have four surfboards and six guitars. I've got all this external stuff. But you know what sobriety has really given me that scares me the most? It's given me the ability to feel my feelings. I can be angry and not run and get loaded. I can be sad or scared and not run and get loaded. And I can be happy and not run and get loaded.

The thing is this: communication. Feeling alone is what takes us out. We know we're not alone, but we also know there's no one who can make it better. It has to be a spiritual battle. The drugs are the final manifestation of the shadow, an unknown lower self. I see the shadow eating away at someone, and the next week, they're dead. I saw it with Christian, and it scares me.

I make so many mistakes. I have so many blind spots. What I do when times are difficult is get support. I don't go it alone. I have the ability to call up people and say, "I need help. This is hard." I don't do that perfectly. I keep coming back to getting support and working through it.

I've got this buddy of mine who says that the coolest thing about recovery is we all don't have a bad day at the same time. You have a bad day, and you call me. When it's my turn, I'll call you. That's how it works. That's the magic.

No More

By Sonny Mayo

I reach out to those who wade in black tar.
I pay the tolls, and I salve their scars.

Cinching the knot with one more twist.
They wander far and blind in parasitic bliss.

I offer them pleas of unified strength.
Their hungry eyes scream 'til the plunger
hits depth.

"This is it," they insist. "The last time,
for sure."
As the tide pulls them down, they trade *one*
for no more...

6

CHRISTIAN HELDMAN

"Rain When I Die" by Alice in Chains

In the Native American Klickitat language, *yacolt* means "haunted place" or "place of evil spirits." That's where my sisters and I grew up, in Yacolt, Washington off the I-5 corridor near the border with Oregon. It was where the insidiousness of my addiction began.

My father, Jerry, was mentally ill. If I had to guess, probably undiagnosed schizophrenia or perhaps some sort of drug-induced psychosis. He had hallucinations and delusions of grandeur. Once, I found my dad lying in the road, out of his mind on drugs. Mom wasn't home. I had to bang on the neighbors' doors to get help, to get him out of the street. Even when he wasn't using, he had hallucinations but would not get a diagnosis because of his paranoia.

My father was both violent and extremely bright. After he stopped using drugs, he became overly religious. He raised me on a heavy dose of the book of Revelation from the Bible. A kid doesn't need that kind of doomsday upbringing, but the expected coming of the apocalypse fit with the eeriness of our "haunted" town.

We were the poorest people in a poor town. Because of his

mental illness, my dad didn't always work a lot. I had shabby, hand-me-down clothes. I was bullied. My sisters and I didn't always get along. We saw violence from our father. When our mother went to choir, us kids would play war. I remember once one sister had an ax, and the other had a burning log. They chased each other around, ready to do real bodily injury. It seemed normal. It was normal for us.

I could have used a drink at, like, five years old. At eight years old, I started smoking weed with a neighbor family. I wanted to change how I felt. I was looking for an escape from reality. I needed to escape from the way my life was.

The first time I got drunk, it was blissful. I acted the fool and had a great time doing it. I was eleven. I woke up, and I couldn't wait to do it all again. It was a very present thought to have fun without consequences, and that's how it was at first.

While my father had mental health issues, he also might have been one of the most talented musicians I have ever known. He owned a jazz coffee house in Seattle and would play with the greats. He played upright bass and piano. As a young child, I lived around live jazz music before the family moved out of Seattle. My dad brought famous jazz musicians to his club: Miles Davis, McCoy Tyner, Herbie Hancock. He'd been housed and played music with African Americans when he was in the Air Force. He liked them and didn't accept the segregation and oppression heaped on them. The police associated the people he brought to the club with heroin. He was getting harassed by police, which made him put more emphasis on the club. This was when I was still very little. He used amphetamines to work his day job, then go to the club at night.

I idolized my father. Though he made no money, he was one

of the greats. The famous jazz musicians he played with said he was a genius, but he didn't have the business acumen to succeed, and the mental illness kept him from making a living. I was in awe of his raw musical talent. It made some of the sting of the abuse fall away. On the other hand, it amplified some of my feelings. My musical idol fell short in the area of fathering.

I started my musical career as a drummer. My dad bought me a kit when I was five. By eleven, I was a decent rock drummer. I continued with drums but switched to guitar at thirteen. I liked to be out in front, and a guitar was more portable than a drum kit.

Things got bad at home. My dad and I had a big blowout. I ran away and started living with a neighbor. My parents sort of abdicated responsibility. At first, I thought it was going to be cool living with this guy. He let me smoke weed with him. But he was a Vietnam vet and had PTSD from the war. One night, he smashed my face into a table, putting my teeth through my lip. He taught me how to burglarize homes. He started me on a life of crime, and I was well on my way to prison by my freshman year in high school.

Then I got a reprieve. My cousin came to visit from Seattle and saw the mess I was in. He called his mother, my aunt. She moved me into her house in Seattle.

All of a sudden, I went from total poverty to upper-middle class. I lived in a big, nice house, was bought fancy clothes. The transition was a challenge. I was good-looking and, suddenly, I was well liked. Now here's the strange thing. The kid who introduced me around the high school I went to created a persona for me. He told everyone I was a cool guy from California and a karate expert. I had never been to California and certainly didn't know a thing about karate. I became popular quickly, but I felt like a fraud. I was wearing a mask. Inside, I was still a poor, bullied, poverty-stricken, beaten child.

Alice in Chains started at my high school. I was in drum class with the original drummer and bass player. At the time, I didn't know they'd become a worldwide sensation. They were just guys I went to school with.

What I noticed is that when I got to my aunt's house, I laid off all the drugs for a while. I hung out with the jocks and preps at that school. We would drink but no drugs. Alcohol was still a social experiment—until it wasn't.

I slipped into a severe depression at fourteen. I'd sit in a chair, curled over with my arms around me, rocking. I learned later that I was someone who didn't want to deal with reality. I was damaged goods already. I knew it. You could put me into this beautiful home, put me in nice clothes, introduce me to successful kids, but I'm still the same person inside.

I started gravitating toward the rebel dudes. They looked like they were having more fun. I started getting into trouble here and there. Right before graduation, the wheels fell off. Though I was invited by three girls, I never made it to prom, and I didn't graduate. Shortly after I should have graduated, I cooked up a cup of mushroom tea and put on an album by Boston. The tea and the decibel at which I played the record made the photographs skip across the mantle. My aunt came home and asked, "What's that smell?" She knew I was high. She shook her head. It was the last straw. She kicked me out.

The Seattle music scene was flourishing. It supported my anger, my lifestyle, and the debauchery I was waiting to get into. One of my friend's girlfriends was dating Pearl Jam's guitar player, and I started hanging out in that scene. I started playing with a lot of musicians who were huge grunge artists. Musically, I fit in really well. I wouldn't trade those times for anything. It was a good experience, but I was very lost. I was using multiple substances. One night, cocaine and alcohol. Another two or three days, methamphetamines. This kind of excessive drug use rattled my brain and perhaps kept me from being part of a band that might have been something.

I met Kurt Cobain. I found out details of his life that I really resonated with. He grew up in a small town not far from the small town I grew up in. His father was a struggling gas station attendant. He grew up in poverty and was exposed to religion at a young age. Then he released an album and became one of the most famous people in the world. I related to his story.

I got to rub elbows and play in rooms with members of Soundgarden, Alice in Chains, and Pearl Jam. A lot of the people I played with are no longer living. Drugs rob us of everything: popularity, fame, stardom, and eventually life. Sometimes when I'm working in a treatment facility, I'll see a teen or an adult with a Nirvana shirt on. Kurt Cobain is their hero. They'll ask, "Do you think Courtney (Love) killed him?" No. I don't. I think depression and drug addiction killed him. I think he was miserable because he felt the powerlessness of being unable to get off the drugs, and he got a gun and blew his head off. I know that because I have known that feeling.

I was a late bloomer with opiates. I'd done everything else. I was twenty-seven and in my prime. I was getting to play with these guys who were rock stars. That's when I was introduced to smoking heroin. It was the perfect drug for me. Heroin gave me the peace of mind I was looking for. All the answers I was looking for in drugs,

I found in heroin. It shut down all the noise. It was like lying on a cloud and having God massage my temples.

While it's legal now, the laws on marijuana were once strict in Washington, but were lax in Vancouver, Canada. There was a lot of marijuana being grown there and brought into Washington. A friend of mine was working for some retired Hells Angels. Now, by "retired," I mean they weren't riding around on motorcycles with long hair. They were wearing business suits and buying houses and big-boy toys up in the mountains. I met them through my friend, and practically overnight, I became one of the biggest distributors of marijuana in Seattle.

What that business brought was an immediate influx of mass amounts of cash. There were weeks when I was making fifty thousand dollars. At the same time, this kid was bringing black tar heroin over to my house. It was the devil's timing. I was making huge amounts of money that I didn't know what to do with, and I was taking drugs that took the pain away.

I smoked that heroin for three months straight. Then one day, that guy didn't come over. I didn't have any heroin in my system all day. When I woke up the next morning, I had huge pupils and was absolutely pouring sweat. I didn't know what was happening. I had never taken a break from heroin. From the first day I started smoking it, I smoked it every day. I walked to my buddy's restaurant and asked him, "What's wrong with me?" He said, "You're dope sick." My father's jazz musician friends had told me, "Don't mess with that heroin. It's evil." Now I knew what they were talking about.

Without the heroin, all those worries and concerns that were drowned out all come flooding back, a thousand times what they were before. I was nauseous, freezing and then hot. I had diarrhea and vomiting. It's like having the flu times a thousand. Everyone I know who's sober says that the closest they got to using is when they were dope sick. You feel like you're going to die, but you have to suffer through it. Here I was, twenty-seven years old with a lot of money and no desire to suffer through anything like that. Now I knew what the problem was: lack of heroin. I decided not ever to be without heroin again. That started a year-long run.

My "friend," really a codependent drug buddy, said, "Why are you wasting three hundred dollars a day smoking heroin? If you do it this way," he said and brandished a needle, "you'll spend fifty a day." I let him stick a needle in my arm. Of course, that fifty dollars a day is only for a short time. I was soon up to three hundred dollars a day, and now I was shooting. It was a massive escalation of my drug use.

It all had to come to an end. For me, the high-living days stopped abruptly through a bust. One of the big distributors from Canada came down, but he wasn't careful. The police were on to him, and I got caught up with him. I had to get an attorney, and though I got out of that mess, I was now on law enforcement's radar. That put a stop to the huge amounts of money I had been making. I burned through the cash I had. I didn't know what to do with money. I was trying to buy people. I had good friends, but I felt like I had to buy people. What I learned is that when I tried to buy people and their affection, they respected me less.

The real start of my downward spiral was when the money ran out. When you don't have money, the consequences of addiction kick in. I started lying, cheating, and stealing. When that didn't support me, like any good, tough junkie, I went back to live with Mom and Dad. By my early thirties, I was running the streets of Portland. That's when I started to hear about detox. There were detox centers I could go to when I got too dope sick. I was introduced to recovery there. I'd be in this detox in a hospital gown, shuffling down the hallway because I was so underweight and weak and on heavy doses of benzodiazepines. They'd say, "OK, it's nine a.m. We're going to have an H and I (hospitals and institutions) panel." And I remember, like, five guys coming in and telling us about recovery. I'd see these guys who had their lives together. They seemed happy. They were free. The women who came in were smiling and attractive. I'd hear how someone went from a street-level junkie to having a happy life. They had years clean and sober. They had things in their lives that were super positive. I wanted that.

I'd like to say that the first time I heard these stories, I joined the club. I didn't. I went to detox about ten times. But it did introduce me to the recovery community. I knew there was a place I could go get help.

Every time I left detox, I thought I was fixed. I had no desire to use. It's easy to have no desire to use when you crave the freedom of being outside. It's also easy when you have a mind clouded with Valium or Librium. But as soon as I smelled the fresh air and the pills wore off, I was off. I couldn't stop using heroin.

Eventually, my sister in San Diego said, "Come down here, or you're going to die." It worked out because she had a plan. I got on methadone, and I got weaned off of heroin. I was on methadone for over a year. Once I ran out of the methadone, the withdrawals kicked in. It was uncomfortable. I was given a Suboxone pill by a friend. Fifteen minutes later, I was like, "Let's go to the bar!" I was high. A short time later, I was back on heroin.

A friend of mine who I knew from Portland came down to San Diego. He'd played in a band, The Jesus and Mary Chain. I knew him from detox. He was a bad alcoholic, the kind that blacks out and pisses himself when he's drunk. He called and let me know that he was sober six months. He and a friend took me to a twelve step meeting. I was sick, dripping snot, and after the meeting, I was surrounded by a group of guys who basically didn't let me out of their grip for months. That was the first time I followed suggestions about recovery and got clean. People were willing to help me with no motive attached except to see me get better.

I'm like forty at this time. I got into the work of dealing with my childhood traumas. I put some time together, over three years totally clean. I got the semblance of a normal life back together. I had a car, home, a beautiful significant other. And I relapsed after three years. Why did I go out? What I've come to learn is the reason I went out was that I was ungrateful for what I had. I was not grateful for the people in my life, for the people who had helped me. My ingratitude created a serious lack of connection with a Higher Power. I was running the show, and I ran it straight into the ground.

Right before I relapsed, a buddy of mine, Brandon Parkhurst, said that with my musical background, I might be a good fit for Rock to Recovery. Rock to Recovery was just getting off the ground in San Diego, and there was a huge buzz around the project. He said, "I'm going to bring you in on this." He saw potential in me.

When I relapsed, I was using for four months. Brandon tried to help me get sober again. I was lying to him, shooting dope in his bathroom. I literally lost my mind. I was mixing all sorts of drugs. A couple of guys who owned a sober living place were trying to help me out, and they'd call me, but I was completely insane. They said they'd help me, even in that state, but I had to make a ninety-day commitment.

I was suicidal, in a sober living facility, sweating into a pleather couch. There was no nursing staff, no drugs to make the detox more comfortable. It wasn't even really a sober living facility, just a room in a guy's house that he was renting out to guys like me. I knew there were firearms in the house. One morning at around four, I was sneaking into the basement to get a gun to shoot myself. I got a call from my mom. From 1,200 miles away, she said gently into the phone, "You just woke me up. Stop it." It would be a miracle if that happened one time, but it happened several times in that detox. My mom's connection to God is the reason I lived through that detox.

I stayed in that house. At one month, I re-evaluated. I was lost and heartbroken from the loss caused by the wreckage of my actions, but I stayed. One month turned into two and then three. When I got to the ninety-day commitment, I knew that I didn't want to go anywhere. I had started doing odd jobs and felt productive. I was in no hurry, and my friends were agreeable to me staying on. I started doing hot yoga. I was going to meetings every day. I had a sponsor. My life started to turn around.

At six months, I went back to my apartment. I cleaned it out, painted, and changed my life. I remember thinking, "What was my hurry?" I thought I had all these reasons to get back into my life, but that hurry to leave treatment, structure, and support was what was taking me out. I lost everything I put in front of my recovery.

Rock to Recovery came back into my life. Once I had six months sober, Brandon gave me an incentive. "You know, once you have a year clean, you can join us in Rock to Recovery. You'd be great at it."

I got to ten months sober. I was doing really well. I had a job that had some purpose. I was caring for someone with a traumatic brain injury and was learning patience through that job. That was an important skill because, at ten months clean, I started to shadow Brandon in his Rock to Recovery sessions.

It was hard to sit in these groups and not participate. I watched Brandon, and I knew I could do the job. I could help with the lyric writing, the guitar part, the piano part. Most important, I could relate to how the people in the groups processed their feelings. I watched how excited people who were non-musicians got picking up an instrument for the first time, learning a little part, and finding the music inside themselves. I watched as their faces lit up when they performed and then heard the recording. They were bona fide recording artists on SoundCloud! For one song, you're your own rock star.

People tell me that I've got a generous heart. Maybe. I know I have a soft spot for the low-bottom junkies, the teens who have been bullied and abused. Sure, I give people a meal or a place to shower. That was given to me. Is that kind? Seems to me it's simply doing the right thing.

I have grown so much working as a musician with Rock to Recovery. It is a job, and at times, we get people in our groups who are super sick and are suffering, but once the music comes on, they're literally dancing in the middle of the room. I get to see the clients' love for music. It's a great vehicle to help people recover. We work with people with addiction and trauma. I get to see the healing every day.

On Christian's Death

"Drugs rob us of everything... eventually life."

—Christian Heldman

Christian died of a heroin overdose on November 28, 2018. When Wes told the company on the text feed, I couldn't believe it. I called him and shouted, "That did not happen!" I was in San Diego doing some work with Brandon Parkhurst. We intended to work together that afternoon, and when we were done, I thought we'd invite Christian to have dinner with us. That dinner would never happen.

A month before, in late October, Christian and I had been together for an event in San Diego. He had been terse with me, almost rude when he picked me up from the airport. As we drove to dinner, we talked about the somatic healing work we were doing with a Core Energetics branch called "Radical Aliveness." I told him that I couldn't stop crying in the work. "I don't cry at all," he said. I found that odd. He had so much to cry about but couldn't tap into those emotions. The trauma of his early years still gnawed at him. We related to each other through trauma. We each knew what it's like to be seriously abused.

It's likely that he had already relapsed, perhaps on meth, when we were together that October. He was thinner than usual and grumpy. Christian was a light when he was sober. Having experienced so much unkindness, he had chosen to be exceptionally kind. But I wasn't around him enough to see the warning signs. I chalked up Christian's irritability to a bad day.

Two days later at Wes' birthday party, Christian performed one of my favorite songs, "Running to Stand Still" by U2. I sang along with him from my seat, floored by the talent I saw in that performance. He had that rock star energy. The lyrics of the song end talking about overdose. I didn't know he was foreshadowing his own death. Was he reaching out for help?

Christian called his sister Kat the night he died. He sounded awful, and when she asked him if he'd relapsed, he admitted that he had. He was afraid that he would lose his job with Rock to Recovery. He was concerned about all he'd lose if he came clean about his using.

"We can talk about that in the morning," Kat told him. She told him how much she loved him as she talked with him on the phone while he walked to the little guest house she'd just redone behind her home. When she wished him a good sleep, she was happy that he was going to rest.

His death wasn't suicide. Christian had no intention of stopping at Kat's house. He didn't plan to die. He just took too much.

The family thought that perhaps Christian had taken fentanyl. It's easy to overdose with fentanyl, but the toxicology report said that he had taken heroin, codeine, and methamphetamine. The codeine was probably in cough syrup. The autopsy showed that though he was only forty-nine, Christian had late-stage emphysema. His body was giving out from decades of drug addiction. His heart was bad, and his lungs were shot. Although he died of an overdose, he probably was close to death from pulmonary disease. No one knew how sick he was, including him. All anyone knew was that his cough was horrific, which we attributed to long-term smoking and vaping.

There was already fluid in his lungs when he took his last dose of heroin. It was too much. His body just couldn't take it. He likely died very quickly. Brandon saw his body. He said it looked like Christian was praying.

This is a cliché shared in twelve step programs: We all have another relapse in us. We may not have another recovery.

Music alone can't save us. It's connection that brings us through. Christian wasn't able to choose connection. Every one of us who knew him in Rock to Recovery is heartbroken.

—Constance Scharff, PhD

ADDICTION

The Scope of the Substance Abuse Problem in the United States

Each year in this nation, well over 150,000 Americans lose their lives to alcoholism and drug abuse.[4] Substance misuse has soared during the COVID-19 pandemic; many people find it difficult to find addiction treatment and recovery support.[5] These are the statistics, but statistics don't illuminate the depth of suffering represented by the numbers. Every number signifies a family torn apart.

It is estimated that there are twenty-one million Americans currently struggling with substance abuse, but only a small percentage (studies suggest between 11 and 13 percent) will receive treatment.[6] [7] The consequences of substance abuse are severe. Drug overdoses are expected to remain the leading preventable cause of death for Americans under the age of fifty.[8] [9] Overdose deaths far exceed the number of deaths from car crashes, and opioids are involved in more than 60 percent of overdose deaths.[10] Overdose deaths will likely reach an all-time high during the COVID-19 pandemic.[11] Deaths from drugs obtained illegally are on the rise, but 80 percent of those who die from opioid overdose began their use with a legitimately obtained prescription.[12] Alcohol abuse alone causes in excess of eighty-eight thousand deaths a year in the United States, with 2.5 million years of potential life lost.[13] Those lives cut short forfeit the positive experiences and connections that might have otherwise been possible.

The drugs available to Americans are getting stronger and are more likely to cause overdose than in the past. Fentanyl use is up over 540 percent in recent pre-pandemic years.[14] There has been a sharp increase in overdose deaths from synthetic opioids, particularly fentanyl. All states and communities are having difficulty facing the problems addiction brings, particularly opioid abuse. It is no overstatement to suggest that substance abuse is decimating our communities.[15]

These statistics, however, don't tell the whole story of what is happening in our cities and towns. Those who suffer from addiction do not do so in isolation. These are real people, our friends, neighbors, and family members, who are connected to us. Every parent of young children who dies leaves those children to family or the foster care system. Impaired caregivers disrupt children's natural development, causing immeasurable suffering and obstacles to a healthy life. Flip the coin, and parents watch children who had promise degenerate into sad and helpless individuals, killing themselves on installment or outright by accidental overdose or suicide. Where substance abuse is rampant, crime and ill health follow. Communities with substance abuse problems often see increases in everything from property crimes to hepatitis rates. Substance abuse is no longer an isolated crisis of the ghetto or poor communities; the death rates of young people in middle-class and affluent families are on the rise.[16]

It is not likely that the problem will improve in the near term.

Although there has long been bipartisan support for addiction treatment, funding allocated to major drug treatment legislation has lagged. Add that to the efforts to undermine the Affordable Care Act and defund Medicaid, and the result is that there are fewer and fewer treatment options available for those who need them. Burr Cook, executive director of Balboa Horizons in Costa Mesa, spoke to this point when interviewed for this project. He said, "I think access to care has always been limited by resources or lack of resources. The landscape has changed in recent years because addiction treatment is more driven by insurance companies than the medical profession. We see limited stays for residential treatment becoming the norm, and we see more emphasis on outpatient therapies."

All over America, instead of expanding access to treatment, treatment centers are closing. Furthermore, as unscrupulous treatment programs have abused the system with body brokering and billing exponentially beyond value, coupled with insurance companies aggressively slashing reimbursement rates beneath validly billed value, it's a perfect environment for more deaths and hopelessness among those seeking quality care and an opportunity for recovery.

The stories in the addiction section highlight the impact that music can have on those in early recovery from substance use disorder.

7

LISA

"Bad Guy" by Billie Eilish

My family is not a stereotypical American family. I'm the youngest of four brothers and sisters but lived as an only child. All my other siblings are half-brothers and half-sisters, so they weren't really raised with my parents. I grew up in an immigrant Iraqi Jewish family. I'm first-generation American. The family was very well off, but it was also absolutely nuts, which probably led in part to my using.

I had a very, very rocky upbringing. I was a terrified child. I saw a lot of physical and emotional abuse growing up. I was always very scared. I had no one to go to, to share my feelings with. My homelife was intensely isolated. I was the victim of verbal, emotional, and physical abuse.

I had learning disabilities. I also had ADHD and was depressed. I remember during the teacher-parent conference when I was only eight, the teacher noticed my learning disabilities and tried to make my family aware of it. She suggested I get an evaluation and ultimately probably medication. My parents opposed it. That meant I was always an F student.

Because I did so poorly in school, I would be "disciplined." The abuse was horrific. I was always talked down to when I got bad grades. Grades were important, and I didn't measure up.

I knew without any friends or support, I had absolutely no escape anywhere. I had maybe one best friend during my early years. I would see other kids get to go out to play with friends and have sleepovers. I didn't have any of those experiences. I had a strict father who wouldn't let me stay out past 9:00 p.m., let alone have a sleepover. I was very sheltered. Meanwhile, I was an American kid. I was searching for affection and escape. That's really what I wanted: to get out of that house and feel loved.

I was trying so hard to grow up and be a mature adult. I remember when I was ten or eleven, I used to have a lock on my door, and I would pretend that my bedroom was actually my own apartment. I set it up to where I had my phone and would pretend to come home and throw my keys on the side table. I wanted to feel like it was really my own so that maybe I could be safe there, away from the family.

We didn't have a TV type of family; we never sat down and had dinner together or talked about what was going on with us. It was more like I got home from school, ate a snack, and waited for my father to get home, when I had to hide. My father would come home an hour or two later, and he would just sit and watch TV. I would try to disappear so that he wouldn't be angry at me for any reason. That's just the way it was.

Drinking was my initial escape. I had my first drink when I was maybe eight years old. It was at a New Year's Eve party, and there were Jell-O shots. I didn't know there was vodka in them, so I took the whole tray of Jell-O and ate it. I felt horrible! I was dizzy. I was throwing up. I didn't like the way alcohol made me feel.

I don't think my family knew I had eaten so many of the Jell-O shots, and I was sure not going to tell them, but the next morning, I was still throwing up. I was probably alcohol poisoned; they thought I had the flu or a stomach virus. It was the worst experience. That was the first time I had any alcohol.

When I was ten, my best friend had a cigarette, and I tried it. My parents were smokers at that time. I used to hate the smell, and I would despise it when they would smoke in the car with me in the back. But at the same time, I used to break my pencils and pretend they were cigarettes. I was obviously imitating behavior that I saw as being grown up, like it would get me there faster. I just knew I had to grow up and get out of the house.

When I was twelve, I was sexually assaulted. There were a lot of repercussions from that. I had a crush on a guy in school. He sexually assaulted me, then flipped it on me. I was completely confused. Because I liked the sex so much, I almost felt like I allowed myself to do it, even though it was definitely forced. But what happened was the whole school found out. He told *everybody*, "Oh, she did this and this." All of these rumors were going around the school. Suddenly, being the victim of a sexual assault turned, and I became a whore. They labeled me a whore.

I had no one, nowhere to go. I had no one to reach out to. The experience reinforced my isolation. I walked through the school with the reputation of a whore. I was afraid that my family would find out what people were saying about me. Even teachers were coming up to me because they heard the rumors, and I'm like, "No, that never happened. I don't know what you're talking about." I couldn't trust any of them. At the same time, I was screaming for someone to help me, but I couldn't open up.

I wanted to leave school, change districts. Beverly Hills schools are a closed community. Rumors spread, but they don't leave the community. I thought that if I could go to a different school district, I could outrun my reputation. But what could I tell my parents? How could I ask them to allow me to change schools? No, I couldn't tell my parents anything. I suffered alone. Girls talked about me as I passed them in the halls, and I could hear it. I would have lunch in the bathroom stalls because I was embarrassed to come out to the yard during recess.

By the time I got to high school, everyone already knew who I was. I was tired of being emotionally beaten and embarrassed and humiliated and labeled. I knew I was always going to be hurt more unless I protected myself in a shell. I had a very soft heart, but I built a hard, slick exterior for a shield. I started hanging out with the kids nobody fucked with. That's where I needed to be so that nobody would fuck with me either. Those kids were the stoners, the addicts, the fighters, the gang members, the thieves, the ones who ditched school. My goal was to be in that group. The kids no one fucked with would be my protection.

When I was in ninth grade, I smoked weed for the first time. I don't even think I inhaled. I just did it to act cool, to run with the cool kids, run to the alleys behind school and have people see me doing something so cool and hard. Weed to me was a sign of independence and defiance.

I started dating the main guy in that group of delinquent kids. The first time I had sex with him was also the first time I tried meth. I was fourteen. I didn't know what to expect, but a girl in the group told me, "Oh, you're gonna lose weight, and you're gonna look beautiful." I was a chubby girl growing up, and I was always made fun of because of that. I'm like, "OK, I'm in high school. I can try this."

The first time I tried meth, I didn't really care so much about it. I preferred weed or alcohol. I would take some liquor to school in a water bottle and drink during PE. That was my MO at that time. But the next time I tried meth, something changed. It was the most incredible feeling. I felt like I had found what I'd been looking for: escape and control over my life. Meth was empowering. I lost weight. I was a social butterfly. I didn't give a fuck about what anyone said about me. I reached out to people that I never thought I would have the courage to reach out to and hang out with. It was the most liberating feeling, so good that I couldn't believe it wasn't legal. Something that gave me so much should be available to everyone! That was the high I ended up chasing for the next fifteen years.

All of a sudden, I was getting straight A's in school, and it felt like I had arrived. Finally! I was even graduating on the principal's honor roll. Using was a part of every day, but there weren't any real consequences. It felt kind of good being sneaky, meeting a drug dealer, and getting my week's supplies because that was what I needed. It was making me a better student, doing me good. But by the time I graduated from high school, I kind of felt that I might have a problem, and I didn't wanna start college as a drug addict.

I went to a doctor and told her that I was using meth to get me through school. She was like, "Oh, well, you're self-medicating." I thought, "OK, 'self-medicating.'" I could handle that word because it seemed scientific. As a substitute for meth, the doctor gave me Adderall.

I had never tried Adderall. She started me at thirty milligrams, which is a high dose. I freaking loved it! It was the same effect, if not a little stronger than meth. So I started doing Adderall just before I graduated from high school. I got the group of friends I was hanging out with to do Adderall also. We were always high on Adderall and Red Bulls. But no speed, no meth. This was legal. It was medicine.

As I said before, I was dating the leader of our group. He was six feet, six inches tall and my first love, my savior. We were together for eight years after we met. But he got arrested. Often.

It was a problem for me that he would bounce in and out of jail. I didn't do well when he was in jail. The second time he got arrested, I had a nervous breakdown. I didn't know what to do. We were together every day and then had no contact. I thought I was losing my best friend. When my guy started doing time, I started getting heavy back into meth again to feel better about his being gone. By the time he got out that second time, I was a full-blown meth addict, and my addiction was out of control.

For some reason, I needed to tell my dad and mom that I was using. We had a family therapy session, and I told my father I needed help. That was the first time my parents put me in treatment. But I didn't know what treatment was yet. I saw it as being in a home with other girls, doing a little group therapy. I even texted my dealer just to keep in touch with him: "Hey, just wanna say hi. I'm doing all right, you know. I'm in this group home for a little bit." But I had no intention of understanding sobriety or learning how to be clean.

I was there for three months, and I was clean. Then my

boyfriend got out of jail again. We were right back together. He started using, but it was heroin now. I started using again too. There was nothing to stop me. I hadn't learned what I needed to in treatment.

Me and him eventually broke up but never lost contact with each other. I genuinely loved him. Still, I moved in with another guy. I had this full-blown meth habit, but he had no idea. He didn't even know what meth was. I had a double life. I would come home to him and go to bed and sleep and eat like I was healthy and functioning, but I was doing meth all the while.

When I wasn't physically with that boyfriend, I was out getting high, finding dope, getting dope, making sure I had dope. It was hard. I had a job. I had to be presentable, not look like I'm a meth addict while I was working with elderly people. I lived this double life for a long time. But my addict behaviors were all there if anyone knew what to look for. I was explosive. I was resentful. I was always the victim; everything was everybody else's fault.

When he ended it with me for another girl, I went completely mental. I was going to make him suffer! I decided to slash my arms in front of him, and I did, only I was just so fucking dumb at it. I started ripping the skin on my arms with a dart. I knew I was out of control. I didn't want to die. I wanted him to hurt.

I knew I needed help. I decided to go into a residential program in Israel where I could do six months of treatment. My sister lived in Tel Aviv, and she had told my parents about it. They agreed I should go there.

I slept the entire flight to Israel; I was so drained. The residence was on a kibbutz, and let's just say it wasn't up to my standards. Oh, and I fucking hated everyone. They placed me in a crappy room. I was super offended. I was already like, "Why am I the one that has to be in the shitty hotel? I deserve to be in the Hilton or the Sheraton." My sense of entitlement blossomed under my addictive thinking and desire to use.

I fought almost from the moment of my arrival the reasons I was in the middle of nowhere with these people. "Why do I have the seediest room? Why am I bussing tables? Why can't I be at the bar?" I hated being in Israel. My sister wouldn't have me in Tel Aviv. She made me stay in Eilat, at the far end of the country. I was certainly out on my own but found myself wanting to be closer to family.

It took two weeks for me to get kicked out of the program. The coordinators wanted me to leave Israel, but I had already started shacking up with a guy, so we found an apartment, and I ended up at a pub out there for three months. I didn't tell my family I got kicked off the program. I didn't tell anybody, but at some point, my parents called my sister, and I guess she told them what happened.

I wasn't on drugs in Israel, but I was drinking heavily. I was working at a club. I had thought that moving to Israel, the change of geography, would help me, but I missed home. I certainly didn't wanna be in Israel anymore. It was hot. It was expensive, and I couldn't tell my parents that I needed money. As soon as they found out that I was no longer in treatment, my parents brought me home. The same day I arrived in LA, I went to my dealer's house and got my drugs, so I was happy again.

I needed money for my drugs, but I couldn't get it from my parents, so I started stealing. Of course, I got caught. That was a turning point for me. I didn't want to go to jail. I made a decision. Before I was sentenced, I decided to go to the CLARE Foundation and give recovery a genuine chance.

I walked into CLARE on July 2, broken, destroyed, and high.

I saw all these girls waiting down in the pit. I immediately started with my excuses: "I don't wanna be there. I hate meeting new people, and I especially don't like girls." We had a Fourth of July barbeque, and I went on and on about how I didn't wanna do this. I wanted to go hide. But I didn't leave. I was there for ninety days. It was the best experience of my life.

The first thirty days, I was on complete lockdown. I was bound to the facility and only got to do a store run like once a week. I started making friends, and I wanted to be with them. When I was approaching thirty days, I'm like, "All right, maybe I'll just stay for sixty days and then go home." After I got to sixty, I'm like, "All right, I might as well just stay for the ninety days."

I had a counselor there who became my mentor. She saved my life. She absolutely saved my life. She talked to me every day. She listened. She understood. I needed validation because I was never close with my mother. My counselor cared for me more than I cared for myself. I even wanted her to sponsor me until I was able to get a sponsor elsewhere.

I was in treatment three days when I found Rock to Recovery. I remember I was wearing one of those lightning bolt sweaters, and I was scanning the room looking at the guys. But I didn't wanna play an instrument. I didn't wanna be there. I wasn't interested in recovery yet.

Sonny led the group. He walked over to me and was like, "What's your name?" I said, "Lisa." And he was like, "Hi, I'm Sonny" and then he hands me the microphone. I was like, "You gotta be kidding me. I'm not gonna sing." My voice is raspy, and I wasn't feeling well. He said, "Well, Janis Joplin had a raspy voice, and she fucking rocked." It was the right thing to say. I love Janis Joplin, so I started writing lyrics. It was awesome. It was one of the best experiences I've had. It made me come out of my shell. Sonny recorded the song and told us it was on SoundCloud.

Even though I don't like my voice, I wanted to hear the song, but I wasn't allowed to have my phone. I couldn't listen to the song until I got phone privileges. Still, it was an amazing experience to be able to connect with my bandmates, to do something that I never thought I'd be able to do: write music, write lyrics, and put everything I felt on paper. What I felt turned into a song.

I wanted to go to Rock to Recovery every Friday. Sonny believed in me enough to put me on the piano. He wanted to hear my lyrics. And it was fun! We were just messing around. That was the atmosphere, that everyone's having fun with some really serious stuff. We didn't have to be too serious even if what we were singing about was serious.

Sonny allowed me to write whatever I wanted to write. I got to see what I was feeling on the page. Everything I was feeling was authentic. I experienced a lot of pain and sadness. Sonny didn't judge me for writing any of that, just gave me the opportunity to say how I really felt. If I wanted to say, "I want to stop treatment," he wouldn't judge me for feeling that way. He made it OK for me to have those feelings. It was normal for someone like me to want to quit sometimes. I wanted to run out of there many times, get high one more time. He made me feel that it was OK to feel that way and that I didn't have to take that action. I could sing about it and not do it.

This was a life-changing experience for me. At home, I was ridiculed or punished for feeling things that were very normal. Sonny made it OK for me to feel the way I did. It's OK to have messed up. It's OK to have lived a dark lifestyle. But it was time for me to change. Everything I did was OK. It was going to be the launching point for my transformation. Without failure, there is no success. Now I work at a rehab. I've taken a whole life of using and chasing, manipulating, lying, fleeing feelings, and facing jail time into a place where I help other people. It makes me feel good to help one other person the way Sonny helped me by taking my struggles and turning them into motivation to do better.

That first boyfriend, who I still love, is out there using, but I'm finally on the other end of the spectrum. I know there's absolutely nothing I can do for him. I can do what I can do, and then there's a point where it's not up to me to help him. His recovery is in his own hands.

When my life changed, everybody who's involved with me, their lives changed also. I have become a different person. I am patient. I'm not so volatile. I'm less explosive. I think before I speak. I try to listen more than I talk. I do charity work. I love animals. I have a sponsor. I'm working through the issues that I had as a child. I show up to work. I show up for my family. I show up for my friends. I take trips with my brother. I go to concerts and festivals. And it's amazing!

One important change for me is seeing that my family is getting older. I love my father now and would do anything for him. I don't want to use again because I don't want to hurt him. He loves me too. I'm very emotional when I think about him leaving or passing. My recovery has allowed us to build a different, loving relationship.

I'm staying clean also because I'd like to be a mom, and I'd like to have kids. I was always told true love comes from good health and the people around you. I'm not looking to escape my home, my family, or my life. I have aspirations, and though some days are hard, I have a star that I'm aiming for, and there's nothing stopping me from getting there.

Plastic Gods

By Joey Alberici

(verse)
Lilly, you grow through the white-driven
snow
toward the man in the dark
who has stolen your spark.
Where'd you go? Nobody knows.

Starlight, you shine. Plastic gods can't
provide
what you really need inside.
I won't ever leave you dry.
Are you there? Somebody cares.

(chorus)
Oh, Lord, even if they're all wrong,
I'll find the strength to belong. Oh, Lilly,
face the sun.
Starlight, even if they're all right,
I promise you I'll walk with you until the
job is done.
Shine bright, my teary-eyed Starlight,
come fly with me tonight.

(verse)

Lilly, you thrive on a world that's
deprived
of the Mother's soft touch
and the Man is as such.
We don't know. We'll never know.

Starlight, you shine into the wind-broken
chimes;
out the window you gaze
for the Man who is to save your mortal
soul.
Nobody's home.

(chorus)

Oh, Lord, even if they're all wrong,
I'll find the strength to belong. Oh, Lilly,
face the sun.
Starlight, even if they're all right,
I promise you I'll walk with you until the
job is done.
Shine bright, my teary-eyed Starlight,
come fly with me tonight.

(verse)

Lilly, don't cry! Through the tears we
survive
the cold winter that blinds us
from the warmth of sunshine.
Let it go! It's time to grow.

I'll make you bloom. The false prophet's in
the tomb.
Follow me; I'll be strong.
Into the sunlight you belong.
Take my hand. Life is the plan.

(chorus)
Oh, Lord, even if they're all wrong,
I'll find the strength to belong. Oh, Lilly,
face the sun.
Starlight, even if they're all right,
I promise you I'll walk with you until the
job is done.
Shine bright, my teary-eyed Starlight,
come fly with me tonight.

*Joey Alberici wrote this beautiful piece in
Orange County, California. He asked that
his full name be used in association with
this song.*

8

JERMAINE

"Ten Crack Commandments" by The Notorious B.I.G.

Gangsta rap was my music when I was a kid. It made the scene sound great, and I wanted to be part of it.

The first time I got exposed to that great music was in the late '80s, when I was six or seven. I remember LL Cool J. I remember Afrika Bambaataa and the X-Clan. I remember NWA, EPMD, Public Enemy with Chuck D and Flavor Flav. I remember these artists on television too. "Yo! MTV Raps" was a show I used to watch. My first cassette was LL Cool J's *Walking with a Panther*. It was '89 or '90. From then, it was The Fat Boys. It was the movie *Disorderlies* on VHS. When we moved to Long Beach in 1992, it was Dr. Dre's album *The Chronic*. Everything in my life spun around that music, and I really dug the lifestyle it was about.

My mom was a single mom, and she did her best to shelter my brothers and me from trouble and danger, from street life. She especially tried to keep me away from that because she knew I wanted to be involved with some heavy stuff like I was listening to, and I was going to have it. But my mom, she did good by me. There was no trauma at home or anything like that. Everything was normal, and she did her best to keep it that way. My mom gave us love and as much protection as she could.

When we moved to Long Beach, I was ten. Long Beach is diverse, and I grew up in what felt like a normal way, with a lot of diversity and interaction with a lot of cultures. Long Beach is not primarily white or black or the other. You have black culture, which was where I fit. You have Hispanic culture. You have Asian culture. Where I grew up in Long Beach was pretty much safe. My mom made sure of that. Some parts of Long Beach were bad. I know the local swap meet and supermarkets got broken into. And the Rodney King riots got down to Long Beach. I was a kid, and I was so excited. I said, "Mom! Mom! They're rioting and looting!" She said, "Come stay in the house!" I wanted to go join the excitement. She wanted me to be safe. That's what it was like for me as a kid.

Music, though, that always got my attention. My first obsession ever was music. I remember at the swap meet they sold these black snapback caps with the green chronic leaf on it. I saved my allowance until I had enough to go down there and buy one. *The Chronic* album promotes weed, liquor, drugs, women, the fast life, street culture. My mom was not about that for me, but she sure knew what the leaf meant.

I tried to sneak the hat into the house. My mom was sitting on the couch when I came in. She said, "What's that in the bag?" I just tried to go upstairs. She said, "No, let me see." She pulled the hat out of the bag, and she's like, "Oh, no," and she took some type of a sewing instrument, took off the leaf, and handed me back the hat. I was resentful that she damaged the hat I had saved my allowance to buy, and that was the start. No one, not even my mom, was going to tell me that I couldn't emulate the lifestyle of hip hop and rap.

I had seen it on television, and it was the thing for me to be into. At the time, that lifestyle was a staple of Long Beach culture. It was the street life. Dre and Snoop were artists who were heavily influential, and I was all in. I went further into the music. From the ones I started with, I moved to Bloods & Crips' *Bangin' on Wax*. Then it was Method Man's *Tical*. I bought Wu Tang Clan. Then there was Ol' Dirty Bastard from Wu-Tang Clan. Then it was Mack 10, *Based on a True Story*. That music, that lifestyle, they were what I wanted.

When I was around twelve, I started using. It was the natural progression of getting into the lifestyle.

I was in junior high school. My cousin was smoking strawberry-flavored bidis, which are leaves that had flavored tobacco in them. They are terrible. They're banned now. But she wouldn't let me smoke her bidis with her because she felt like I was gonna tell on her. I got resentful of her, so I took a newspaper, and I rolled it up and smoked it like it was a cigarette. I was like, "I can't smoke your bidis? I'm gonna show you how I can smoke!"

From there, I experienced alcohol. I'd had my first sip back in the late '80s, but I didn't take off with it because I was so young. Liquor was common in the household. Our mom would sip wine, or she'd go to her sister's house, play cards, and sip liquor there. Every so often, once in a blue moon, she would say, "You want some?" I would have the smallest sip of a wine cooler or the Zinfandel. It wasn't a problem. Later, because I was trying to emulate the lifestyle I wanted, I started to drink.

I started smoking weed in ninth grade. On one particular

night, I already had been drinking. I knew I was gonna smoke weed because I went and hung out with an older brother of mine. I was like, "Yo, Mom, can I go out with my older brother to the high school basketball game?" She was like, "Yeah." In my mind, I was like, "Whoa" because this brother and I, we're like oil and water. He had his crew of friends. I had my little crew. I was being steered in the right direction; he was already in trouble, getting locked up and the whole nine. He was a youth, so it was the juvenile hall, but he already demonstrated his direction, and I hadn't yet. And so I was like, "Wow! My mom's letting me go out with my brother?" I was super nervous and anxious.

Once I smoked, everything was funny. I laughed the entire night, and I was like, "Yeah!" I'd been hearing about weed, especially listening to Dre and Snoop. I had the physical effect, and it was amazing. After that, I smoked weed for the effect of the first experience I had with weed. But even when I switched to other stuff, it was a good high, but I never got nothing like that first experience, nothing was ever that good again, and it became a problem because I was always looking for it.

In 1998, I moved to Antelope Valley and lived with my brother, his wife, and their children, while my mother worked. He wasn't as strict with me as she was. I could get away with a little bit more because he worked a lot. I started going astray into the street life. I was already engaging in criminal activity, which came along with the alcohol and the weed smoking. I was never in a gang, but we all had the same sort of lifestyle.

I wasn't into the criminal activity to support my habit. I just wanted the lifestyle, and the using came with the lifestyle. I had been drinking for years, but the weed got the better of me in high school. It got to a point to where I started ditching school a lot because of it.

The lifestyle got me arrested. The first time was when I was in eleventh grade and then again right after high school, when I was in for real jail. Getting in trouble became habitual. I ended up in prison twice.

At first, jail was no big deal. It went with the lifestyle. I got slapped on the wrist, did maybe ten days, then went back into the lifestyle. It was like having bragging rights. Then, at the end of 2000, I went back again for burglary charges, and this time, they sent me upstate to Delano. That was my reception penitentiary. Next time, I went to Susanville, where they gave me half time on my sentence. That could have worked out well for me. I went to fire camp, and I had fun there. But when I came back down from fire camp, I came back with contraband. I had some lighters and stuff because I wanted to make money on the yard. I was caught with the contraband, and then I didn't get to go home as early as I thought I might. Instead, I was sent to Chino. I did most of my remaining sentence there.

In December 2001, I ended up in Inglewood as part of an early release program. The halfway house I was placed in literally faces Century Boulevard in a section of town known for prostitution, drugs, and gangs. At that point, I was nineteen, and all the other guys in the halfway house were from state prison. Many were older and full-fledged addicts. They were going out, copping meth, and bringing it back into the program.

The first time I got offered meth, I turned it down. I was in that halfway house. I went to the room next to mine to ask the guy a question. He was sitting in his room with a pookie pipe, and he and another guy were torching; man, they were blazing! I'm like, "Whoa, what's that?" and they're like, "Meth. Here, you wanna hit?" Based on just the glass pipe, I thought, "That shit does not look fun at all." They're in there fucking tweaked out. Their eyes are all bright and big, and I'm like, "Nah, I'm okay." I drank my whole stay there, but I didn't do meth.

I was having fun through all that. I did not see where my life-style was taking me.

When I got out of the halfway house, I went deeper into the criminal lifestyle, and I was smoking more weed. That's when I started using meth. I didn't like that high much because meth keeps you alert and awake, but the guys I was hanging with, they were lacing meth inside of the weed. I wasn't screening guys the way I should have. I'm like, "Yo, I wanna get high, man." That's what it was like, and I took what they had.

Sometimes they put sherm (PCP) in the weed. I'm already paranoid because of the lifestyle; sherm made me super paranoid. I think I'm about to die. My heart gets to speeding up as it's beating, and in my mind, its like I only have a minute or two to live. It's crazy. You would think with the meth and sherm experience, that'd be sufficient to make me quit, but it wasn't because somehow quitting meant that I'd be turning my back on the lifestyle, and I didn't want to do that.

Finally, that changed. My mom was a big part of why I wanted to quit. I'd come home and see my mom all worried because I was gone for days at a time. She was awake that whole time, worrying about her son. I saw how scared she was, watching my problems escalate from liquor and weed to meth and sherm. It wasn't fun at all to see my mom hurt like that. It got to a place where I really saw how I was being drawn into bad experiences. It wasn't fun anymore, and it made my mom cry.

I saw where my life as going, and I wanted to stop using, but I didn't have the power to stop. The twelve step literature talks about powerlessness. I would tell myself, "OK, Jermaine, you're not gonna drink or get high today. You're not." I would leave all of my money at home and go out. But I would end up with these same friends, and I'd drink and smoke with them. They looked like they were having fun, and I told myself that I was having fun too, but deep down inside, on the emotional-spiritual level, I was really low.

I had my first child when I was twenty-one. I wanted to be a father to her, but I didn't stay home with the mother of my child and do the family stuff. I hung out with my homeboys. When I came home close to noon, I got into bed. I was drunk and high all the time. Maybe I'd do the daddy thing for an hour or two, but after that, it was back to the homies. I could see the cycle and what it was doing to my life, but I still didn't have the power to stay away from my friends or not get loaded.

That's what it was like for years.

Eventually, I went back to prison. I caught a case in 2009. I was catching a few cases here and there. The behavior and the lifestyle kept holding me. What changed was that I caught a case that was drug related. That allowed me to be eligible for the SAP program, a substance abuse program, when I went back to the pen for the second time. I went to Wasco reception, and then I went to San Luis Obispo.

I opted for the SAP program because I would get released

forty-two days early, if I completed it. I wanted to get home as quick as I could. I started to hear some things in that program that gave me a new outlook on my behavior and my thinking. I heard some things like the ABCs. They said that your actions become behaviors, and behaviors carry consequences. Hearing things like that, I decided I had to make a change, to take a different action. I recognized there were people who needed me to be better than I was, so I ended up going to treatment in 2011, when I finished my sentence.

I went to a treatment center in Long Beach, but I kept getting written up. There was a guy who was a director in the program who would sit down and discuss things with me. He would show me exactly where I went wrong, and he would suggest a solution. He wouldn't just say, "Hey, man, you f'd up." Instead, he'd say, "It's all right. It's a mistake. Try doing this next time."

In one particular incident, one of the roommates in my sober living facility would eat everyone else's food. I was mad. This guy had a full-time job making fifteen dollars an hour when we were all making minimum wage, which was a lot less. He made the most money, but he's eating all our food. We had a house meeting every week about this guy.

I went to my mentor and explained the situation. He said, "You gotta talk to him, Jermaine." I was frustrated. We talked to this guy every week! My mentor said, "You've got to keep reminding him until he understands." With that, he taught me about having patience and not giving up.

Another time, I was between sponsors when a man came on a panel to speak to us. This guy was an ex-pimp. I was like, "Yo, man, can you be my sponsor?" He came every week, sat down with me and the guys. He had a nice Cadillac. It had pretty pearl paint on it. It had a set of stock rims; they were chrome with some Vogue tires. It would always be washed and waxed. They say to choose a sponsor who has what you want, so I chose an ex-pimp because I liked the car. And, of course, with that motive, it didn't work. I wasn't ready for the message of recovery. I was still looking back at the lifestyle and hungering after it.

Eventually, I met another guy who put his hand out to me. I called him, and we started to work the steps. I had a beautiful experience, but I only got so far into the steps with this guy because I was getting more involved with all the distractions that come along with getting sober. He suggested I get a new sponsor.

I had gone to a few meetings. I heard people sharing. I heard this one particular guy at a meeting in Long Beach. He said something that was super profound to me. He said there's a lot of great one-, two-, three-steppers in the room, but what about the entire product? He said, "What do you have to offer a newcomer who doesn't know how to stay stopped?" I heard that. It kinda crushed my ego because I felt like he was talking to me. I felt like he knew what I had just experienced with the previous sponsor. I went to this guy and said, "Hey, man, you know what? I've heard you share at a few meetings here and there. I like how you carry the message. I like how you carry yourself as well. The truth is, I wanna go through the work with you. I really want what you have to offer."

We worked the steps twice. We did the work, but it wasn't really doing the work that made me stay involved with the process; it was the results that I was getting in my own life. When I did the steps, my life got better. I've been sober since my arrest date in 2009.

Once I really started changing, it has been a beautiful journey because of the twelve step process, knowing people, my life being changed, me being recreated. I ended up working in treatment. That is how I came to be involved with Rock to Recovery, through my work at a treatment center.

Working in treatment, I wanted to get to know all the groups. I have a tech position, operational staff. I'm the first line of defense against a person leaving treatment too soon. It's important for me to know how all the groups run and what they cover so I can help the people in treatment. The title Rock to Recovery did catch my attention. I asked one of the guys who works at the treatment center about it, but he was kinda vague. He said, "Some guys come in and play music for the clients. They do songs." I didn't know what to expect, but I was interested. It was music, after all.

I went to Rock to Recovery because I wanted to check it out. We'd been having some trouble because some residents in the house weren't motivated to be in recovery. They didn't want to participate in anything. I was the kinda guy who tried to provide motivation, so I started to sit in on sessions.

Sometimes because of the house, and losing clients, or moving clients around, or therapy sessions, there wouldn't be as many clients for a full group. And so I volunteered to play instruments and help with the people writing songs.

I was just there to assist as I could. It was hard for me because I'm not a musician, but most of the clients aren't musicians either. That's the beauty of Rock to Recovery. And what I see as I observe is the clients gain interest. Over time, they become more and more motivated. And every so often, there's always that one guy—he wants to write the song, he wants to sing it, he wants to be the forefront guy. I got to see Rock to Recovery become instrumental in helping people change their lives.

What I like about it is it's not the typical twelve step thing. It's not the dynamic of the ordinary treatment stuff. It's not like, "Hey, well, how do you feel?" Or talk about this and that. It's like, "Hey, OK, what kind of music do you want to do, man? OK, that's awesome. What would you want to say? We could put that in a song. You feel like you wanna jump off a bridge? Let's put that in a song."

I have met a lot of the Rock to Recovery guys. Those guys, they care. They really care. And I've seen them for weeks, and weeks, and weeks uplift other guys. I've had clients come in super bummed out and sad, low key, borderline depressed, and they go to Rock to Recovery, and then they're changed. And then they come into the office like, "Yo, when's Rock to Recovery getting here, man?" They're more enthused to be a part of that movement. That really touched my heart.

Now things are changing for me. I'm thinking about my future. I'm currently in school pursuing a math degree. I wanna be able to finish that and be working in that field. I wanna be a math teacher.

Of course, there's always more money to make, quote, unquote, "always." But I don't need rich in financial gain. I want stable, and OK, and content financially. I just want to be happy, joyous, and free. I wanna be able to really hone into inner peace and be useful at helping people in any way, if possible, for positive reasons.

Now I'm working in West Hollywood at a sober living place. When guys come into the sober living where I work, they're coming in with Rock to Recovery stickers. They're coming in with Rock to Recovery wristbands. I'm knowing these guys are coming from all over Southern California, having experienced Rock to Recovery. I tell them, "Hey, look, man, I know these guys." And I show them my laptop. I've got a Rock to Recovery sticker on my laptop. And these guys, they remember Rock to Recovery. That's priceless.

I do wanna let anyone know, especially the guys who are running Rock to Recovery, that they do have a great, positive influence on the people they come in contact with. I know we can't help everybody, but I do believe that we can plant seeds in people's brains. They have done that. And I wanna do that too.

9

RACHEL

"Motion Sickness" by Phoebe Bridgers

I was raised Christian, so I didn't blame God for anything that happened because I know that we have freedom of choice. Everything that happened was just because that's how it is on Earth. People do horrific things, so I hated this world.

I was born in Redondo Beach, California. My mom had me when she was twenty-three. My parents got married right after my mom had me. In an Asian family, that can happen, but not often. Families like mine usually have the wedding as soon as the pregnancy is known, not after the baby is born.

My home had little stability. We moved around a lot when I was very young. My dad is a professional golfer, so he would travel around the country, and he taught students eventually how to play well enough to get into PGA tournaments. We settled in Georgia until I was twelve, and then we moved out to Orange County when I was thirteen. I have a younger brother also. That was the family, and nobody would have thought we had problems. Outward appearances are everything.

I don't have any good memories of my dad. He was a functioning alcoholic. That's how I saw him. But he was an exceptional golfer, so the outside looked really good. It was actually pretty perfect on the outside. Everything that happened inside the house, inside the family, was not to be talked about and was swept under the rug. I grew up with trauma that I didn't get to deal with until I was in the seventh grade. My dad was very violent when he drank. I was aware of that. My brother was aware of that. When my dad drank, he would lose it. Every memory I have of him is of him yelling, or hitting my mom, or something like that.

My parents got divorced when I was in the second grade. From that time on, my mom dated alcoholics and gambling addicts, one after another. She always chose men with problems. My mom's a really codependent person. She couldn't break that habit all throughout my life.

Growing up, I just wanted to disappear. At a young age, about fifth grade, I knew I had anxiety. I told my mom, "I have anxiety. I need medication for it." I don't even think anyone talked to me about that, but I just realized that I was nervous about nothing in particular a lot of the time. I was also very depressed. That combination of conditions, along with my home life, made me wanna die. I wanted to be in heaven with God. I did not wanna be here. I remember one time when I was twelve, I called the cops and told them I wanna go to sleep and not wake up. They took me in on a psych hold. That was our first official recognition growing up that I did not want to be a part of this world. I did believe in God. I always believed in God, and I never blamed God for anything. I love God. It's this world that's awful.

I was unhappy, depressed, I mean really sad all the time. And then in sixth grade, I started drinking and smoking weed here and there. My first day of middle school, someone gave me a weed brownie, and I took it. From then on, I was a big pothead, and I drank daily. I was still able to function on a certain level. I always had good grades, always managed to get things done. I had to. It was expected in my family. And I had seen my dad do it, so I knew what functional substance abuse looked like.

But my mom, we definitely had a really toxic relationship. We could not ever get along. The animosity lasted all my growing up. I think it was when I was in sixth grade that my mom finally decided she wanted to be a mom to me. She was ready. I don't know what changed for her. She had never been available to me before. She was focused on her codependent relationships with men. Meanwhile, I had been traumatized by what I had been through and seen, things I'm not prepared to talk about yet. And I was just like, "You weren't there for me when I needed you, through everything that I've been going through, so I don't want this now!" Her desire to mother me made me rebellious. I did not care for her. I did not like her. Actually, I hated her, so we developed a poisonous relationship with no communication whatsoever. I ran away a lot, stayed out a lot.

Because she was unable to parent me, my mom looked to others to do it for her. She wanted to control me. My mom became a big cop caller. She would call the cops on me for not doing the dishes. Can you believe that? And the cops were like, "We can't discipline your child. You need to stop calling us. There are other serious things going on in town. We can't make your child obey you."

In the ninth grade, freshman year, I was fourteen. There was a neighbor—he was twenty-three—who would buy alcohol for me and all my friends. Sometimes he'd get us some weed but mostly alcohol. Anyway, one time we drove somewhere, and he picked something up. I asked him what that was. He told me it was coke, but it was meth.

My grandparents live in Hawaii, and we visited them a lot. All those years before, all my growing up, I would see Meth Project commercials like "Not Even Once." All those commercials, anytime I was there. So I knew that no matter what, you don't do meth. In my head, I thought of coke as a party drug, and it's fine. You can do coke, and you'll have a good time with no consequences. But meth was a totally different deal. Meth had consequences. I knew that.

I ended up doing meth that night with the neighbor because I thought it was coke. I was fourteen, a kid. I didn't know any better. I didn't know what meth looked like. When I found out the next day that it was really meth, it was kinda like all bets were off. Instead of being afraid, I went to a place of not caring what happened to me. It didn't really matter anymore. I had felt amazing on meth. Meth fixed my anxiety and depression, so I kept getting high.

The trouble with meth is the highs are high, but when I would come down, the lows were too low. I was suicidal a lot when I was coming down, but that wasn't really anything new for me. I was used to not wanting to be in the world. I traded the highs and the freedom from the anxiety, the depression, and the trauma in my past for the lows where I tried to kill myself. I thought I'd be with God soon enough. Why not enjoy the highs as much as I could?

Within two weeks after I started doing meth, I got sent to juvenile hall for the first time. My mom and I got into a massive fight.

I was charged with assault and battery, though I wasn't guilty of that. My mom was chasing me, and I kept trying to get her off me. She'd pin me down. I couldn't breathe. I had been doing meth for seven days. But that's not what got me in trouble. I was losing it. I was angry, saying stuff I probably shouldn't have, screaming at the cops. If I'd kept my mouth shut when the cops were there, I probably would not have been sent to juvenile hall. But I definitely had a mouth that day, so I ended up going to juvenile hall for the first time. I spent my fifteenth birthday in juvenile detention.

After that, I kept going in and out of detention. It was like once I got in the system, I was always going back. I did not know how to stay sober. I didn't wanna be home. I'd do a UA (urinalysis drug test) and be dirty, or I'd break my curfew, or I'd just run away from home. Every time, I'd get sent back. I didn't wanna be home, so I'd deliberately do stuff that would get me taken away. I was doing whatever I wanted to, and I experienced a lot of stuff that a girl like me didn't know about. I'd been pretty sheltered from the drug and gang thing growing up. I didn't know there was a dealer on every corner of the street. I didn't know anything about hard drugs, but I found out fast.

One of the things that would keep me in my depression when I was using was that my mom labeled me as bad. She called me a junkie and told me I was worthless, unlovable, a horrible member of society, the scum of the earth. I decided that, OK, I would be all those things since I was already condemned.

I deliberately put myself in really bad situations for a fifteen-year-old. I hung out with guys who were older than me, adults. I mean they weren't necessarily bad people, but I did a lot of things that were not safe for a fifteen-year-old.

I hit bottom when I was using a lot of heroin, maybe two

grams a day. I was slamming it. I was using for about six months. I had gotten sober for a brief period during that time—I don't really remember why—but then I relapsed.

I was done with living. I made a suicide attempt that didn't work out. I kept trying to die. I'd overdose on purpose, but people kept bringing me back with NARCAN. One day, I just gave up on trying to kill myself. I felt like, "OK, I guess I'm not gonna die, so might as well try and get sober because that's the only way I'm gonna be pulled out of the state I'm in." I couldn't die, and I couldn't go on how I was living. I went to detox, and I went through a rehab program.

That's where I began taking Rock to Recovery seriously. I'd met Brandon Parkhurst a few months earlier when he came to a residential program I was in then. I didn't care for what went on in Rock to Recovery. Well, mostly I didn't want to participate in anything, and I certainly didn't want to participate in anything where I might have to feel my feelings. Brandon brings that up a lot, the importance of feeling our feelings. I was definitely in a negative state of mind in those early days of treatment. But, later, I was kinda willing to do what I was told to do, and if that meant doing Rock to Recovery and participating in group, I was willing to try.

In the beginning, I was hesitant. Brandon got me out of my comfort zone. I write poetry. Part of Rock to Recovery is someone writes something, the lyrics to a song, and then everyone else sings or plays an instrument in the band. I wrote song lyrics, and I also have a decent voice, so he convinced me to sing. I'm not really sure what happened, but it somehow became a really good experience, an experience I looked forward to each week.

Brandon is very easygoing, and when he told his story, the whole constant in and out of treatment, the instability, and all of that, I could relate a lot to it. He'd slammed a lot of heroin not to feel his feelings. He'd had people around him die and talked about how it hurt him. That had a strong impact on me. I had tried to die a lot, but I didn't think anyone would care if I did. There were a lot of similarities between our experiences. I also think the mindset I had at that moment was a lot different than before. I was paying attention. With Brandon's personality and the difference of the mindset I had, I became open to taking a risk, as Brandon says, and willing to do the group. Once I made that mental shift, I really got a lot out of it.

Participating in Rock to Recovery was a challenge for me. If I'm not immediately the best at something, I'm not doing it. I'm not gonna make a fool out of myself. If I'm not the best, I won't go there. That was probably why I did OK in school. It was easy for me. Brandon taught me that even if you're not the best, you should still do things that you enjoy. Learning is part of the process of recovery.

Now I definitely have an energetic personality, but I'm an introvert at heart. People drain me. I'm naturally quiet. I really don't wanna talk. I'm not the first person to approach someone. Usually, people have to approach me in order for me to talk to them at all. But I think that whole experience with Brandon allowed me to be a little vulnerable, and that's not something I grew up doing in my family. In my family, vulnerability got me hurt. Brandon taught me that it's OK to share my feelings, that not everyone is going to penalize me for feeling or hurt me if I show them who I am.

Growing up in my family, I was not able to do anything musical, which made me sad. I remember singing when I was really young, maybe seven years old. My mom told me that I had a really bad voice, and I needed to stop singing. So I grew up thinking I had a horrible voice because my mom told me that I did. But I apparently have a decent voice, and the more people who heard me singing, it was kinda like, "You're OK. You're good at this. You're not bad." I told my mom, "Do you realize I grew up thinking that I cannot sing at all and that I should be super embarrassed if someone heard me? You told me I sucked at singing growing up, and you made me think I had a horrible voice." And she's like, "No, you did have a horrible voice, but now you don't." I am learning that I have to go outside my family for validation.

Rock to Recovery definitely brings a fun aspect into my recovery. It's inspired me to do things that I'm not used to, that I haven't done before, or to do things that I'm not really comfortable trying at first. I am learning to be open to new things and willing to try them. If I don't like something, I don't have to do it again. But I learned that I could enjoy things I didn't expect to like.

By the time I left the Rock to Recovery program and rehab, I wished I was not leaving. I've been able to stay in touch with Brandon, and I feel super grateful for that connection. I'm also honored to have him think of me for this book. Telling my story in this way is not something I would have tried before I met him and participated in Rock to Recovery. It's been really cool. I have never had genuine happiness like I have right now.

When I got sober this time around, my perspective on life changed. I grew up having the perspective that my life was a series of horrible events. I really believed in the core of my heart that everything in my life was just bad experience after bad experience, and that made me want to check out, only I couldn't even succeed at dying.

But now I realize, this time around, that, yeah, bad things happen, but good things are happening at the same time. It's not just like life is one or the other. What gets the focus is where I choose to look. I've started looking for the good. It's crazy because once I believed in only the bad stuff. I don't remember any good moments of my childhood, but I know they must have happened. I think my mom took us to the beach and to Disneyland, all this stuff. We went on trips, but I don't really remember anything from them. That's not her fault. I chose to look at what hurt me, not at what made me smile.

I realize that I have a choice. I'm not gonna be a victim to how my life was anymore. I'm going to choose to be happy. I can choose to believe that the world isn't a bad place to be. Some negative things have happened since I've gotten sober that I did not expect, but I just gotta roll with the punches.

When I was using, I knew I wasn't going anywhere with life. My life was in shambles. It was not gonna get any better. I felt like the worst person on earth when I was getting loaded. I would always say that I felt like I was just taking up space. Now that I'm sober, I'm not feeling that way. I'm giving back. I wanna feel grateful for life, not like I want to leave it. That's the mindset I'm working on.

My best friend passed away a month ago. She was a really good person, a better person than me. She had a good heart. No one ever had anything bad to say about her. She was thirty and had a husband and a good family. Her parents were missionaries. Her brother committed suicide, and she lived through that. I recognize that while I always wanted to die when I was using, she didn't plan on dying. I'm still here, so I choose to be grateful and to do something with my life. I wanna make a positive impact on this world before I leave it, and for now, I don't want to leave.

TRAUMA

Responding to Trauma and Therapeutic Outcomes

Responding to Trauma

Trauma response may develop when a person experiences a situation that overwhelms their ability to cope. This can happen in a life-threatening event, such as war or rape. It can also develop over time due to domestic violence, institutional racism, misogyny, bullying, or similar types of ongoing abuse. These situations may surpass a person's ability to cope. Feelings of helplessness may develop. Trauma survivors often experience an inability to feel a full range of emotions, a diminished sense of self, and difficulty connecting with others in meaningful ways. Creating resiliency and providing opportunities for the expression of pent-up emotions are two ways to help trauma survivors recover.

The songwriting process used in Rock to Recovery builds on the idea of emotional upliftment.[17] By first writing the lyrics and then singing what comes up as a group, participants are often able to bypass the trauma responses that keep them from speaking up. We have had individuals write lyrics for others to sing, and individuals who sing what they cannot say in conversation with a therapist or confidant. Whether it's expressing taboo feelings, such as those associated with self-harm or suicidal ideation, or responding with rage to a situation in which a person was victimized, songwriting can be a powerful response to trauma.

Rock to Recovery participants report many positive outcomes from participating in our program. Here are some of them.

Replacing Stigma with Hope

Stigma is defined as disgrace. Many of the people we work with feel ashamed of their mental health difficulties. Family, friends, and community may judge them as "bad." Stigma is one of the leading reasons why trauma survivors do not reach out for help. It is a problem for those with eating disorders, when frustrated family members say things like, "Why can't you just eat?" Those with addiction very often act out in ways that hurt others. They can lie, steal, and cheat to get the drugs or alcohol they need. The feeling of disgrace often amplifies because of the shame they have for behaving poorly. Stigma creates obstacles for access to effective treatment.

Hope is the antithesis of stigma and the foundation of recovery. In the songwriting process, each person is critical to the project's successful completion. The song will not come together if any- one fails to do their part. If the lyricist doesn't write or the percus- sionists don't play their beats, the song cannot be created. Being a valued part of a creative project is part of how we replace stigma with hope. "I matter" and "I can do something worthwhile" start to become an inner mantra for those who write songs in Rock to Recovery sessions. Building the concept that each person's life and recovery matters is an important piece upon which to build positive clinical outcomes.

Teamwork—the "We" of the Band

There are many different types of therapeutic music programs. Most involve listening to music. We form a band. Ours is a group process. We do this for a specific reason. Alone, we most often do not recover. Together, we have a fighting chance.

The "we" concept in Rock to Recovery is borrowed from twelve step programs. The founders of Alcoholics Anonymous (AA) understood well that when left to their own devices and best thinking, suffering individuals often make poor choices. Scientists can now explain that this is in large part due to the way the brain is co-opted by addiction, and it's similar with trauma. But even given the neurological changes that reinforce addictive behavior and trauma response, when individuals work cooperatively and in support of one another, their success in recovery surges. This "we" idea brings the individual not only out of isolation but also into communication and connection with others who can begin to become a community of support.

Creativity

Mental health concerns suck the joy out of life. Creative pursuits can help bring the joy of living back to an individual who is suffering. Writing and playing music engages almost every part of the brain, including the pleasure centers. When depression, trauma, low self-worth, or other issues overtake mood, engaging in creative acts can help to shift neurological processes, allowing one to experience pleasure that had previously been unattainable.

Accomplishment and Pride in a Job Well Done

One of the common themes among the stories in this book is that after participating in Rock to Recovery, people feel a sense of accomplishment and pride in a job well done. This is not a customary feeling for those who are in treatment for addiction, trauma, or other mental health issues. The ability to follow through on important activities decreases as our problems grow. The Rock to Recovery program focuses on recording the song. In the time allotted, something is created, and it's usually of a lot higher quality than participants think it's going to be. Finishing a job and feeling proud of their work is an integral part of the recovery process.

Expressing Feelings

Music is one of the oldest tools used to help people express feelings. In tribal or aboriginal communities, musical interventions are typically based around drumming or rhythmic clapping/foot stamping. Therapeutic drum circles are used across the nation in many settings. Other types of music interventions involve a therapist playing a song or certain type of music and an individual talking about the feelings the music evokes. There are groups in which one or two people bring in a composed piece and play it for the group.

Our songwriting process aims to bring the group to unified catharsis, the release of emotions together. Songwriting is an incredibly useful way to express pent-up feelings through both lyrics and music. Sometimes the mood during a session is light, and participants might want to write a song about the awful oatmeal that was served at breakfast or the tedium of listening to people talk about their feelings in process groups. These songs can be fun and help participants bond around shared experience.

At other times, a member of the group will need to share something quite dark. In these cases, the check-in topic helps people process hot-button issues on a personal and unique level. That information then gets brought into the song as a unified and supportive awareness. This can be developed in a way that supports recovery.

While Rock to Recovery doesn't have any hard rules, the basic concept is to bring solution into the song. Often, the verse can be really dark; facilitators let the participants express whatever they want. For example, in one of the songs written with a veterans' group, one of the participants was allowed to do a spoken-word bridge that was well over a minute long about how she had thought about killing herself the previous day. For that to become a positive release, the dark lyrics are followed up with a chord change that lifts the energy to a brighter vibration, and chorus lyrics are written that often are a direct response to the negative thoughts or feelings addressed in the verse. In the aforementioned song, when the vet talked about her suicidal thoughts, the chorus was "but my dreams are bigger than my nightmares," as a solution to the issue of suicidal ideation.

Participants have definitely written songs that were intended to get anger out, with lyrics like "Don't fuck with me!" There are no hard boundaries, but facilitators try to avoid a song without any hope in it.

Finding the balance between expressing difficult emotions and following it up with solution and hope is an important role of the group leader. The leader creates the container for the safe expression of emotions and also has to uphold boundaries that support recovery. When that is done appropriately, individuals can use songwriting to express feelings they might not discuss in other ways, and that information can also be used in other therapeutic settings to work through and find a healing expression for those emotions.

Faith

Connection to something greater than ourselves is part of the end of isolation. Many people who are part of Rock to Recovery in treatment settings have unresolved or difficult feelings about spirituality or God. Some feel abandoned. Others are angry. Still others are embarrassed by their behavior and see no path to redemption, especially if they have been involved in criminal acts, raised in oppressive environments, or seen horrors in war. Writing, playing music, and singing can help resolve those difficult emotions and engender a feeling of connection to the spiritual aspects of life. Making music can help one develop or rekindle a sense of wonder about life and the world.

Positive Reinforcement and Encouragement

Positive reinforcement and encouragement begin at the very start of the session. As each session starts, there is a check-in in which participants can express something solution-oriented. A session might start with a question like "What do you want to gain from this experience, and what do you want to leave behind?" Another prompt used is "Is there something you've lost that you want to reclaim in your recovery?" As people focus on these questions, they are humanized to themselves and others. Instead of focusing on their negative traits or problems, they can begin to think about goals and potential positive outcomes. Participants develop hope as they define how they want their life to change. That positivity and focus on solution can then be put into song.

When a participant shares vulnerably from a real and honest place, the group leader responds with "You're rad!" Most of the time, the participant's face lights up. It may have been a long time since they were loved. Now, when walking down the streets near any of the treatment centers where Rock to Recovery is used, you will often hear program alumni yell out, "You're rad!" when they see a Rock to Recovery facilitator.

Facing Fear and Stress

If you are not a musician, being asked to form a band and write a song can be a frightening prospect. The individual is being asked to do something they have never done before. This mirrors recovery. The individual doesn't know how to live without their "problem" or how to navigate the changes caused by physical limitations or altered psychological circumstances. Radically transforming one's life is daunting, if not terrifying. Writing a song allows one to face a fear in a safe environment. By experiencing success in a small way with a songwriting collaboration, the individual can apply that skill and experience in other settings.

Neurological Change

Writing and performing music activates almost every part of the brain.[18] This is important because it shifts the entire neurological system. The addict's desire or need to use is the prevailing force in the brain. The addict thinks about using until the force becomes so strong that they must get their drug. This is true even after a period of recovery. Trauma survivors face repeated intrusive thoughts, body memories, hypervigilance, and other experiences that rob them of their ability to be present. Engaging with music interrupts these neurological feedback loops. Imagine the songwriting process as a jolt to the brain. Additionally, the pleasure centers of the brain are activated in the songwriting and performing process when feel-good chemicals are released. The individual feels not only pleasure but relief and release from the thoughts that overwhelm them. By creating music, individuals are changing their neurological processes for the better. Making music makes the brain healthier.

Stay Engaged in Treatment

Perhaps the most important outcome we have in Rock to Recovery is that participants report that the program gets them excited about the recovery process sooner and willing to stay engaged in their treatment process longer. Let's be clear: on its own, writing and playing music does not cure any mental health issue. We are part of a therapeutic process that promotes change. However, Rock to Recovery is engaging in a way that other activities are not and often provides the reinforcement of a natural high when the session is over. This combination of fun and emotional release is a reason participants stay engaged and in treatment. Longer engagement with treatment is shown to improve long-term outcomes for individuals in a wide variety of treatment programs. Especially among those with addiction, trauma, or suicidal ideation, we know that longer treatment stays have a direct correlation to lives saved.

Rock to Recovery's outcomes are particularly good with individuals in recovery from trauma. The stories in this section describe how music can help people move from post-traumatic stress to post-traumatic growth.

10

SARAH

"Don't Walk Away" by Meg Ammons

In 2016, I had been sober for seventeen years. I thought it was for good, as "permanent" as any sobriety can be. I wanted to be sober and was doing everything a person should do to stay that way.

In September of that year, I was on the phone with my sponsor when this guy knocked on my door. He had an ankle bracelet on. He pointed to it immediately, started to give me the shuck and jive. He was just out of prison, trying to get back on his feet. He said he understood if I wanted him to go away, but would I please listen. He asked to do some yard work. Drugs are what put him in prison. He said he was scared he was gonna relapse—yadda, yadda, yadda. Well, I'm hooked. I'm a social worker, and there's something so familiar about him; he's the kind of guy I worked with before. I thought, "I'm gonna help him." My sponsor heard all this from her side of the phone, and she said, "Why don't you let him do some yard work?"

So I did because my yard was a mess. He was there for several days. I told him I was seventeen years sober in a twelve step program and asked if he'd ever tried one. I offered to introduce him to sober men. It was like I had a project! He was perfect for me to be codependent with; he began to develop crisis after crisis. The more trouble he got into, the more I was drawn into his life.

I kept right on helping him. I coached him for job interviews. I loaned him some money. I was totally hooked. I thought this was a guy I could fix.

After several weeks, he asked me if I would take a short road trip with him because he needed to face somebody he'd wronged in his past. Would I support him? My gut screamed at me, "This probably isn't a good idea!" I ignored it.

I should have known better. I was a trained and licensed social worker. Moreover, we are told in twelve step programs not to work with people of the opposite sex. We certainly all know not to get into a car with someone we don't know well. But I thought, "I'll go." I desperately wanted to help this guy. I needed a good accomplishment.

As soon as the car door lock clicked, I knew I had made a terrible mistake. He abducted me. I was missing for two and a half weeks. He immediately began using drugs, crack primarily. He'd probably been using before he kidnapped me, but I had been blind to it. I wanted to see him in a particular way, and I did.

I don't remember the first time that I used. I remember distinctly saying to him when he tried to pass me the crack pipe, "You know I don't do that shit. I'm in recovery." He must have drugged me. There's a big blank spot in my memory. The next thing I remember is using around the clock.

He was in human trafficking and knew how to get me to comply with his demands. We used a lot of drugs, especially crack. He shot me up with all sorts of drugs. He shoved pills in my mouth. He made threats against my son. He knew where I lived. He also knew where my son was when he was staying with his dad. He knew where my son went to school and what time they let out. He knew where my ex lived, what his truck looked like. He made threats against everyone I cared about. He took my phone. He coerced me to go into banks and take out cash withdrawals against my credit card. He forced me to give him my savings. All the while, he kept me fucked up. I was terrified that he would hurt my son.

Then he started introducing prostitutes into the mix. He needed to demoralize me, to make me feel less than human. They were getting hotel rooms on my dime. I'd never seen anyone blow through money that fast. There were a lot of twisted sexual situations I was forced to watch and participate in. I don't want to go into detail about that. It was horrific, and it was nonstop, but I had no power to pull away from it. I knew if I did, my son would be harmed or killed.

After two and a half weeks, I caught a break. The last day that I was with my abductor, he was getting more and more tweaked out. Every time he used, he would get extremely paranoid. Once, he sat watching the air vents with a gun in his lap for hours. He was waiting for somebody to come through an air vent in the hotel room. He was that level of paranoid. He was absolutely out of his mind, and by that time, I wasn't too far behind him.

He accused me of stealing a bunch of money, which was my money anyway, but I had not touched it. I woke up to him choking me and slapping me around. He sexually assaulted me. Then he forced me, at knifepoint, to take a shower. He shoved a bunch of Molly and Percocets down my throat and dragged me off to another hotel room, where he made me pay a pimp and his prostitute five hundred dollars to rape and beat me. He said I needed to learn street justice.

For the next several hours, I was left in the hotel room with that couple while they partied and laughed and talked about what they were gonna do to me. Out of nowhere, he showed back up and declared, "Before the fun gets started, let's go out drinking. Sarah says she's an alcoholic, and I wanna see her drink." They dragged me off to a bar, where he lined up a bunch of shots in front of me.

That was my limit. My experience with the twelve step programs wouldn't let me do it. Sure, I had been smoking crack for two weeks straight, but there was something about seeing those shots lined up that gave me strength. I refused to drink the alcohol. I was like, "You can't make me do it. I won't do it. You cannot make me do it. I refuse to drink the alcohol."

He was angry and threatened me. He held a knife on me under the table. I said, "I don't care what you do to me; you can't make me do it. I'm not gonna do it."

He dragged me out to the car, leaving the other pimp and prostitute inside. He shoved me into the car and drove us to a Walmart parking lot. It was almost midnight by then. He held the knife to my throat. He cut me a few times on my arm. He made me pray because he said this was the end and I needed to make my arrangements with God.

For me, it was a spiritual experience. I thought to myself, "This is it. I'm really gonna die tonight." I felt an overwhelming sense of peace. I looked back over my life, and I thought, "It's all OK. It's all good. It's OK."

As I looked at him and waited for him to kill me, he nodded out. His hand with the knife dropped into my lap. I couldn't believe my luck. He had overshot the mark with the drugs he took and had nodded out!

I grabbed my pocketbook and hauled ass into the Walmart, screaming. The employees were trying to lock the doors, but I pushed my way through. "He's trying to kill me!" I screamed. They parted like the Red Sea. Of course, they called the cops.

When the police arrived, he was still nodded out. They arrested him and charged him with six felonies. I was taken to the hospital and then to a domestic violence shelter.

At the shelter, I met with a counselor. She said, "You're the victim of human trafficking." I looked at her like she had a third eye. It had never occurred to me. Even with all my training, I hadn't seen the signs. She said, "There are five steps involved in sex trafficking a person. The trafficker gains your trust. They start you on drugs. They desensitize you to sexual situations. They rape or beat you or have someone else do it. Then they put you on the street." I was stunned. That was exactly what had happened to me, except I hadn't gotten to the street yet. That would have been the next step, assuming he didn't kill me first.

My case was transferred to the human trafficking department within the police department. That experience was almost as bad as being trafficked. The police didn't seem to care about me at all. All that mattered to them was getting the data they wanted off my phone. My abductor had used my phone to set up plays for prostitutes and to buy drugs. Instead of working what I thought they should—my abduction—the police wanted to know if I had seen this girl or that girl, what gang members I'd interacted with, and so forth. I was like, "All of them." Because they were not interested in my abduction and experience, I felt expendable.

The police asked me why I didn't leave. They pushed hard. I could have left. I wasn't tied down. I didn't have an answer. I know now that it's the result of the training. Sex traffickers beat you and keep you loaded and train you not to leave, but I didn't see that at the time, and I couldn't explain it to them.

Because I didn't leave, the police developed the idea that I went willingly with my abductor, that we had a Bonnie and Clyde kind of thing going on. That wasn't the case, but a lot of people saw the situation that way, including my son's father.

I was almost charged with several crimes. The police gave me no sympathy. I see that as a lack of education on their part, but then I could only keep saying that I wasn't a willing participant, that I was just being used. Eventually, they accepted that I was a means to an end for this guy and didn't charge me with any crime.

I lost everything as a result of my ordeal. My life savings and my sobriety were gone. I agreed to allow my son to stay temporarily with his father while I got back on my feet. I don't know that he will ever be returned to me. My son's father doesn't allow me to see my son at all. He doesn't trust me or believe that I was abducted. I lost my business; I couldn't continue as a practicing social worker until I got my life in order. I wasn't capable of being a counselor at that point. In two and a half weeks, my life was gutted.

Going back to twelve step meetings was hard. I'd pick up a newcomer chip, and people would ask, "Where have you been?" When I said, "Abducted and forced into the sex trade," they didn't know what to do with that. It's an outside issue in most twelve step programs. I didn't fault them, but it made me feel completely alone and isolated and disconnected. I retreated.

In December 2016, the guy who abducted me went to court.

The DA offered him a deal without even talking to me. She dropped four of the six felony charges and lowered the last two to misdemeanors: assault on a female and possession of drug paraphernalia. He got 150 days. That man destroyed my life, and he wouldn't even spend six months in jail.

I snapped. I cussed out the DA in the courtroom in front of God and everybody else. Then I called the detective and ripped him a new one. Finally, I called the dealer that my abductor used. I still knew his number by heart. I let him have it too. None of it changed anything. It didn't even make me feel better.

My life was over. I didn't care what happened to me. Inside of three months, I went through over twelve thousand dollars buying drugs and picked up a felony possession charge.

My brother forced me to go to treatment. He knew I would die if I didn't get help.

I agreed to go to treatment for thirty days, but I had no intention of getting clean. The place I initially went to in Georgia suggested that I go to California to a center that specializes in sexual trauma and substance abuse. I needed specialized treatment because I had been sex trafficked, and this was a place that handled cases like mine. I allowed myself to be shipped off to a beautiful facility in Newport Beach, but I had lost my faith and my hope.

A short while after treatment began, I had to return to North Carolina for a court date. My sobriety was gone within two days. I spent over five thousand dollars on drugs in less than a week.

I don't know what came over me, but instead of staying in North Carolina and succumbing to addiction, I called the owner of the sober living center I'd been staying at in California. She told me that she, too, had been abducted. Instead of tossing me to the curb, she asked if I would come back to treatment. I agreed.

That's where I encountered Rock to Recovery. I have to say that music has always been a huge part of my life. I hear music in my head almost twenty-four hours a day. I call it Sarah radio. One of the ways I think I coped with my social anxiety is to tune in to that. Like, if I'm somewhere where people are talking and I'm afraid or don't know what to say, I just tune in to what's playing in my head. That's how I get through it.

And I sing. I joke that I've been a professional shower singer all my life.

Even though I knew I could sing, in my family, if you started to toot your own horn, you got dragged down. You were a target. In response, I learned to lay low and "hide my light under a bushel," as we say.

But I could not push away the power of music. Music is a self-soothing tool for me. When I was sober before, every spiritual experience I had was related in some way to music. Somebody would sing something, or a song would start playing, and I'd suddenly understand an idea or spiritual principle. Growth for me always had a relationship to music.

I have to admit, when I was in treatment after the sex trafficking, I was hostile. People would say, "It's gonna be all right," and I'd snap, "How the hell do you know? You don't know if everything's gonna be all right. Sometimes things just aren't fucking all right." I struggled in treatment. I'm a social worker. I had *led* these groups in my former life. I was the head of DBT (dialectical behavior therapy) in the clinic I worked at. I wasn't going to go to DBT classes! My attitude was, "Oh, God, fuck this shit. Been there. Done that."

But Rock to Recovery was different. For one thing, it doesn't promise me anything. They don't tell me that everything will work out. What they do is give me an opportunity to express myself. It helped me start to see some hope. Playing in a band wasn't something I had done before, and it was musical. I grabbed on with both hands. Rock to Recovery was something I could get lost in.

In treatment, before Rock to Recovery, I was suicidal. I saw no future, no purpose. "Why am I here? What's the fucking point?" I'd lost my son, my career, my money, my sobriety. There was just nothing left. But when I encountered Rock to Recovery, it was the one thing that I could look forward to. It was the only thing I had. Every week when Monday rolled around, I'd say to myself, "Two more days, and then I can go to Rock to Recovery."

Because I can sing, I was often chosen to be the singer in our band, but I also turned out to be a pretty good lyricist. I got handed the notebook a lot, and I'd just start writing. It was so satisfying to have a group of people together, most of whom had no musical experience whatsoever, and write a song with them. Everybody plays a part, and collectively we come together and create something awesome. Every experience was magical.

Songwriting gave me an outlet, a way to express what I didn't think anybody else could really understand. Honestly, I don't think most people can comprehend the magnitude of what I've been through. But now I don't know that that matters. What matters is that Rock to Recovery brought me back to valuing my recovery. It gave me something to hold on to and gave me some hope.

The life that I had is gone. The woman I was once is dead. She doesn't exist anymore. With that old life behind me, I had no path forward. But all of a sudden, I was getting positive feedback for my songwriting. I was like, "Wow, I can write songs!" Little by little, a foggy picture of what could be started to open up for me.

Even with that hope, I still had more using to do. I began renting a room from a man who is not in recovery but didn't seem to need to be. He does his own thing. He's responsible. He works every day.

But one day, while he was out of town, I was rummaging through a drawer in the bathroom looking for a pair of tweezers. In the drawer, I found a little baggie with meth in it. I freaked. I called my sponsor and took off out of there. I went to a meeting. But I didn't get rid of the meth. I let it sit there for two months.

Long story short, there is a saying that goes, "Poor me. Poor me. Pour me a drink." I didn't take care of myself. I didn't go to meetings the way I should have. I got hit with some disappointments. I used that meth.

My relapse was like any you hear about. It started over literally nothing. I knocked a glass of water off the fucking table. The glass broke, and water went everywhere. That was all it took. I was like, "Fuck it. I'm gonna go smoke that fucking meth." My response to knocking over a glass of water was to smoke meth. There is no right-sized thinking in the addict's world.

That was two weeks ago.

The next day, I beat myself up over it. "You know better than this! After everything you've stood your ground against, and you just used over a fucking broken glass?"

But here's the thing. Now I know what I want. I want sobriety. I really do. Because I know I will not get my son back without it.

That relationship is one I have a chance to regain, and I want it. I want to be the mother to him that he deserves.

Right now, I am focusing on developing a relationship with a Higher Power. That is the crux of my problem and the reason I relapsed. I lost my trust and faith. Even though I know God's not responsible for what happened to me, I'm still doubtful of His love.

I think addiction is one of the most isolating things you can experience. Rock to Recovery broke through that isolation for me. Somebody will come up to me, hold their hand out like a microphone, and tell me, "Sing it for us, baby. Sing it." And I'll start singing. The pain pours out of my heart in those moments. Rock to Recovery has given me back my song. Music is healing me.

11

JORDAN

"I'm Still Standing" by Elton John

The whole time I was growing up, I was sure of just one thing: that I would never be good enough, no matter what I did. Anything I tried to do, there was always somebody better than me. My parents wanted me to be the best, so of course I did too. I wanted to show them that I could measure up.

I went to Catholic grade school. The Catholic ideal, as I understood it, is to be perfect in both thought and deed. I had a lisp, a noticeable imperfection. I believed I needed to get really good grades so that the other kids wouldn't pick on me because I had to go to speech therapy. I was even an altar boy. And I was gay, though I didn't admit it even to myself yet. That was one of the biggest "imperfections" of all.

Kids weren't the only ones to pick on me for being less than perfect. If I brought home a B, my dad would be like, "Why do you have a B in this?" From second grade on, I was constantly being forced to tell him when I was falling short. He made me feel like I wouldn't be worth anything until I was number one at what I did.

I changed my focus from schoolwork to sports. I played baseball, basketball, and soccer. I ran cross-country and did karate. Still, there was always somebody better than me, so I quit. I learned to be a quitter. If I couldn't immediately be the best at something, I didn't see the point in spending my time working at it. I felt like every time I quit something, it was better to have guys disappointed in me because I was quitting than it would have been to disappoint my family and myself by not being the star of the team or the guy with the top grades.

The other kids started calling me names. It was easy for them to do that to me because I didn't stand out in any positive way. I was average, easy prey. One of the names they called me was "faggot," I guess because of the lisp. I didn't know what it meant when they first used it, but I knew it wasn't anything good.

I always wanted to fit in, but for me the only way I saw that I could do that would be to be able to brag at home that I was the best at something. Not being able to do that made me really unhappy. Weed was the solution to that problem. When I smoked weed, I didn't care quite so much about failing to hit my goals. At thirteen, I started smoking weed and stealing cough medicine from the grocery store.

My freshman year in high school, I was a good student. I had a 4.25 average. Most people would say I was an exceptional student, but that wasn't good enough for me. I didn't feel like a good student, so I started drinking. Drinking got me a whole new group of people to be with, people who were genuine friends. We drank together, and they didn't care about my lisp or call me names. By that time, I knew what "faggot" meant. I didn't want to be called anything bad but especially not that. I didn't have much self-acceptance in those years.

I liked drinking. I thought it was fun, and I could act ridiculous because everybody else who was drinking was acting ridiculous. We were doing it together. We could even black out from the drinking, and that was fun too. I was safe with these friends, and we were having a good time.

I moved on to snorting cocaine, dropping ecstasy, and taking mushrooms. I started skipping classes to get high. In my junior year, I failed five out of eight classes. I didn't care. I told myself that I was having fun, even though my friends were not following me down this path. Again, I didn't care. I already knew I wasn't good enough; I wasn't special or exceptional. I was accustomed to quitting and to failing. I used drugs and alcohol so that these perceived shortcomings didn't bother me.

When I was sixteen, I got my first job. I worked at an Applebee's. The rest of the crew was older than I was, and they used a lot of drugs, including opioids. What was great about it, as far as I was concerned, was that they were willing to share. Lots of people who do opioids start on them because they were prescribed for illness or injury. They needed them to get out of pain from a surgery or a sports injury or a car accident. Not me! My coworkers were handing out these pills for free, and I started taking them.

Opioids were a revelation for me. I was like, "I like this feeling. This is good."

The problem with the pills was that as long as I was taking them, I was enjoying myself, but if I ran out, I'd get a really bad headache. I'd tell the crew that I had a headache, and somebody would hand me a Percocet, Xanax, or Oxycontin. I'd pop it, and the headache would go away. That went on for about two years.

I just loved those pills. I popped them at first, then graduated to crushing and snorting them. I dug snorting. I would snort anything and everything, from hash to Tylenol.

About that time, I started college. Being a quitter, I quit the first one I went to. I went to a second one and quit that college too. I started losing jobs. The money began to run out. Every time I wasn't high, I felt more and more inadequate. I'd start asking myself who would want to put up with me, because I didn't want to put up with who I was when I couldn't get stuff to snort.

Three days before my twentieth birthday, I was raped. It was devastating. I am not ready to talk about it publicly, but it happened.

I found out I was HIV positive as a result of that assault. I felt completely worthless when I received the diagnosis. Not only was I not the best, I saw myself as one of the worst. I needed something to make me not think about what had happened. I made a decision. "Well, I'm already going to die from AIDS, so I might as well go the whole hog and do heroin." That idea made sense to me. I wasn't getting free pills anymore. My habit was costing a couple of hundred dollars a day, but it wasn't easy to get pills from doctors anymore. You had to get a prescription, but there were fewer doctors who would write them for users, and some were getting arrested. I didn't need to go to a doctor for heroin. I could snort that too, which I found appealing.

The HIV diagnosis really messed me up. I told my mom about my diagnosis right after I got it. I don't know what I expected her to say or do, maybe make me feel worse than I did, emphasize my feelings about myself. Maybe I expected her to tell me how I wasn't good enough to be her son or live or who knows what. Only she didn't do any of that. She gave me support. That first night, I stayed in her room. I couldn't let her love in. I was already an addict, so after she fell asleep, I snorted a whole bottle of Xanax right there next to her. I just didn't care.

Once I started doing heroin, I stopped going to the doctor for HIV meds. That's pretty messed up, when you think about it. I was traumatized from the rape and the diagnosis. It felt like death was coming up on me fast. I thought that if I was going to die anyway, I might as well get it over with and do it on my terms.

I deliberately overdosed on a whole bunch of stuff. I was twenty-one years old and getting dope sick all the time. I thought, "I don't want to deal with life anymore." I didn't want to be dope sick. I didn't want to think about the rape. I wasn't prepared to deal with the treatment for HIV. I didn't see myself as worth anything. Overdose felt like a good way out. Before the drugs could take effect, I got picked up and taken to the psych ward. I was angry with myself. I thought, "I can't even kill myself right."

Looking back, I don't think I was really trying to commit suicide, even though it sure looked like it at the time. I wanted help but didn't know how to ask for it. I didn't know who to ask. I wanted to save face. I couldn't go to anyone looking like I wasn't strong enough to help myself. I think that happens to some people who commit suicide. They might not know how to ask for help.

In the psych ward, they didn't give me anything but Tylenol and Flexeril. I started to go through withdrawal. I didn't realize that's what it was. This time, I was sicker than I had ever been before. At home, I always at least had some drugs. In the hospital, I had nothing. I felt bad. But I didn't see myself as an addict, so I didn't think about what I was going through as withdrawal. I felt a good dose of self-pity. My focus was on getting out of the psych ward and not feeling so bad anymore.

A friend picked me up from the hospital. We started smoking weed right away and drinking. Within six months, I was back on the heroin and using cocaine because the weed and alcohol didn't work for me anymore. I did that for three more years. I lived with a guy who was also on stuff. Every cent I got went up my nose. My family and friends held interventions, but I wouldn't go to treatment. Drugs and alcohol weren't my problem. My problem was being HIV positive and being a loser. I couldn't let anyone know that I needed help with anything. I still wanted everyone to think that I had the potential to be the best at something. I remember once thinking that the only way out was dying; I'd already tried that, but it didn't work. I would have to wait for it to happen naturally. Except that I wasn't dying. I was living on miserably.

I was living at rock bottom. The relationship with this other guy was going nowhere. I was back working at Applebee's, bleeding money whenever I got any. Fortunately, the HIV wasn't worsening despite the fact that I didn't do what was necessary to treat it.

I woke up one day and saw how completely stuck I was. Every morning was the same. I'd wake up, throw up, take some dope, and head for the guy who would sell me more.

Something shifted. I sent my mom a text saying, "I can't get off this by myself." She told me to come over and we'd figure out how to get me into treatment. I think for a few moments I hated admitting that I am an addict more than I hated myself for being stuck all that time. Admitting I was an addict meant I was never going to be the perfect son my dad wanted. But my mom was determined to help. She started calling around. She found a treatment center in Santa Monica that would take me. It was a residential place where I was supposed to stay thirty days, but they kept me for forty-seven days because my detox and initial attitude were so bad. When I entered treatment, I had no intention of staying clean. My goal was to lower my tolerance so that I could go home and start using again.

Part of the detox process used phenobarbital. I was getting a little too much of it, and it gave me a good feeling. The people in the rehab saw that I was a little high and uncommitted to recovery. One day, one of the techs pulled me aside and said, "Dude, if you go home now, you'll be dead in a week or two. You haven't done any work here. You haven't done any of the reading. You haven't got yourself a sponsor. You don't even listen at the meetings. Do you want to throw your life away?"

I could've said yes. I almost did. I had tried to kill myself in the past. But something hit me, and I thought, "No, I don't." I admitted that I didn't want to die.

That was a turning point for me. I stayed in treatment. I got a sponsor. I started working the steps and building a support system. That's also part of why they kept me that extra two and a half weeks. I had started putting in the effort it would take to save my life.

I followed up rehab with sober living and outpatient. That was where I did Rock to Recovery.

I was walking in the hallway when I heard the music. I looked into the room, but it was intimidating because they were playing guitar and had good voices. All I could think was that this was another thing I couldn't possibly be the best at. Sonny saw me and beckoned to me to come into the room.

Sonny didn't ask me to be the best at anything. He asked, "What kind of music do you like?" Everyone likes some kind of music. He made me feel comfortable, part of the group. When I said I couldn't play an instrument, he gave me this little egg shaker thing. He treated me like it was just as important for the group that I shake the egg shaker as it was to play a guitar or a keyboard. For two weeks, I thought I wouldn't go back, but I always did. Even though I only shook the egg shaker, there was a magnetism to the experience that kept me showing up.

The third week, I picked up a clipboard and started writing. It was fun, and I was having a good time being part of the band. Other groups, you had to talk about your issues and listen to other people talk about their issues, and there was all this complaining that dragged me down. When I was messing around with the music, it was a chance to just be me. For the first time in my life, I wasn't using, and I didn't care that I wasn't perfect at this stuff. It was great! I could enjoy myself without being "the best."

I graduated from the egg shaker to a tambourine and then to drums. Eventually, I was on a keyboard. It was all fun, not just for me but for everybody else in the room. It didn't matter if I wasn't an expert at my instrument. We could be ourselves, comfortable with that and with one another.

Music allowed us to have fun. Recovering from addiction is so serious. The music gave us a chance to let loose, to have a good time with other people who were in the same situation as us. We worked toward a fun common purpose. Instead of having to talk about my issues, I could just let go. In that letting go, things came through that I and others had neglected for years. Big feelings. Big problems. And we could let them out together.

What came up for me is that it doesn't matter how good I am at a specific task. As a person, I am good enough, and so is everybody else. I was doing something creative, and it wasn't a disaster! I was part of a group, a team. All of us had real problems, and we were all good, loving people working to heal.

I am a selfish person. Using drugs like I did is unbelievably selfish. I used no matter what the consequences were for you or me. Sometimes even now, that selfish tendency comes out. Rock to Recovery taught me that I don't have to be the most important person in the room, even to myself. I may not be the most talented, the brightest, the best, but I can be a vital part of what is going on, and that made me truer to who I really am.

My healing is happening. I recognized that I hated being called a "faggot" so much because I am a gay man. That, too, is not a defect or a weakness. It's me. I'm learning to judge myself less, especially by someone else's standard of perfection.

I'm in school now to be a drug and alcohol counselor. I'd like to run groups geared toward LGBTQ individuals because that particular community has higher rates of substance abuse than the general population. There are reasons that is our reality, and we need to address them. I was one of the statistics, trying to cover up my feelings with drugs.

I can be an example to others. I am starting to talk about being raped. I am taking care of myself physically, doing what is necessary to slow or stop the progression of the HIV. I am ready to build an imperfect life rather than hurry toward death. We are all imperfect. I want to help people in my community recognize their worth the way I have come to recognize mine.

Together

By The Five, Six, Seven, Eights

Together we can form a group with love.
We can work together as one.
We are all a sisterhood of love.
Put a bit of heart in it for love.

We rise and shine 'cause we're sisters and
we're brothers.
Stand together, working with each other
right now,
Tonight!

Together we can form a group with love.
We can work together as one.
We are all a sisterhood of love.
Put a bit of heart in it for love.

All we have to do is believe.

*"Together" was written by the dancers of
The Pretenders Studio Inc. in Santa Monica,
California. The young people made Rock to
Recovery® a beneficiary of their annual
dance recital in December 2019. To better
understand how Rock to Recovery works, they
participated in a session. Thank you to The
Pretenders Studio Inc. and their service-
oriented nonprofit Dance for a Difference Inc.*

12

DANIELLE

"Numb" by Linkin Park

I was four years old when my dad died of a heart attack in front of me. That was the first time I felt abandoned by a person I needed to love me. I was the only one in the room with him. His face went slack before he dropped to the floor and was gone. It began a pattern I didn't know how to deal with until I entered recovery fifteen years later.

I want to share a happy memory about my dad. It's important to me. We used to go grocery shopping together at Albertsons. Every time we went, he got me a stuffed animal. He was my buddy, my best pal. He protected me. He took me to the park, pushed me on the swings. He fed me breakfast, lunch, and dinner. He watched TV with me. He was the man. What we had together was love, pure love. We were super close. And then he was gone.

My mother was an alcoholic, and she wasn't anywhere to be found when my dad died. The police took my sister, who was ten years older, and me to a shelter. I'll always remember being that four-year-old in the back of a police car being taken to a strange place where we didn't know anyone. We were there until our aunt got custody of us. It took two days. Our mother couldn't take care of us; she was out drinking. I didn't know it until many years later, but she had tried to use the twelve steps to get sober. She couldn't do it. She didn't seem to have the willingness. She died about a year after my father. She was found dead in a hotel room. She had choked on her own vomit and was covered with feces. I have a lot of compassion for my mom now. What a terrible end to her life— to be widowed, lose custody of her kids, and die like that within about a year.

We stayed with my aunt until my mother died. After that, there were a lot of discussions about what was to be done with me. I was little and needed so much attention, and my aunt and uncle were already older. From my perspective, they shuffled me off to be adopted by friends of the family, but my aunt kept my sister. Because I needed too much care, I was sent away. I learned from that that needing help, love, or support was a liability. It got me abandoned again.

The family that ultimately adopted me were friends of my biological family. They were pretty wealthy. My adoptive mom had never been able to conceive on her own. My adoptive dad had been married a couple times before and had multiple older children, but he was open to his present wife having a child to raise. They were in a happy marriage and had a home and open hearts, but I was confused. I needed to latch on to someone to love who was always going to be with me. The only consistent love I had known in my life was from my sister. To me, my new parents were taking me away from my single source of love and stability. Adoption felt like another abandonment.

The crux of the problem is this: I was five, and everyone treated me as if I was a regular five-year-old who had not experienced any difficulties in life. I received no help to deal with grief or trauma or to allow me to understand why I was being adopted. I did my best to go with the flow. I didn't want to be a burden to anyone. I believed I was being adopted out because I needed too much, even though I tried to do my best to fit in, to be lovable. Maybe I thought I might be able to stay with my sister if I didn't need so much, but it didn't work. I was moved along to my adoptive family.

I started using when I was eighteen. My drug of choice was cocaine. Of course, my first substance was alcohol because it is easy to get. I could sneak a beer without consequences when I was young. It was accessible. Ultimately, though, I was a cocaine and marijuana user.

However, before I started to use drugs, I had a lot of emotional issues. One of my obstacles was that I never learned how to process what I had experienced. As a young child, I had received no psychological help. My adoptive parents thought they could shower me with love, give me a wonderful home, toys, and trips. They thought that spoiling me would fix me. They believed that love and attention were all any child needed to thrive. But by the time I got to them, my third family, I was afraid to trust. If I trusted you, you went away.

What my adoptive family gave me was beautiful. Now I am grateful for the home they provided. It was miraculous and wonderful. They truly did the best they knew how to do. But what I

needed more than their gifts was a place to heal and feel safe. I
needed to develop a sense of belonging and security. I didn't know
how to tell them what I needed, and they didn't know how to listen
to me, even if I'd had the words. I needed to talk about my grief. I
didn't have the opportunity. My extreme loss and wounding fes-
tered and grew.

Around sixth grade, I still hadn't had anyone to tell my story
to, so I told it to the kids on the playground. I had to get it out, and
I did, but no kid knows how to deal with what I had been through.
Most adults don't know how to deal with it. I felt lost and alone,
and it showed. Sharing the way that I did got me labeled as weird.
I started getting bullied.

When even my classmates began calling me Orphan Annie,
I had some kind of a psychological shift. I remember distinctly in
sixth grade losing what little self-worth I still had. I stopped caring
where I fit in. I stopped trying to make friends, to be part of anything. I felt like I wasn't ever going to be part of a group. Who were
my family? Who were my friends? Everyone seemed to be in a
temporary relationship with me. I felt too damaged to believe that
anyone would stick with me. I believed in the very core of myself
that there was something incredibly wrong with who I was. And
when I gave up, rage surfaced.

I started being disruptive and loud in the classroom. I started doing poorly in school. I got in trouble. I was suspended for
pouring water on other students' seats and things like that. I didn't
listen. I got angry at home. I became extremely resentful of my
adoptive parents. I went into this "no one loves me; they're not my
real family anyway" fury. My sister had graduated from high school

and gone off to college. She wouldn't be part of my life again for several years. I felt utterly alone.

Not knowing what to do with these feelings, I let the rage drive me to violence. Hate was my central emotion. I hated everything and everyone. I fought with my family constantly, especially my adoptive mom. Nothing she did or said was ever correct. I also hit puberty young, so in addition to being full of rage, I also had all these normal emotional and physical changes going on that I didn't know how to deal with.

My adopted parents didn't know what to do with me, so they had me put on meds to control my violent outbursts. The medications didn't work. They didn't stop my violence, anger, sadness, or emotional upheavals. My emotional upset got worse. I became angrier and more resentful. In addition to hating everything and everyone around me, I started to hate myself.

Finally, my mother sent me to therapy. I have to give her credit; she tried. Unfortunately, I was not sent to someone who specialized in childhood trauma or working with children. Instead, my mom found a therapy office that gave student therapists their hours to become licensed. The student therapists had no experience with kids like me, and every few months, they moved on when their rotation at that center was up. Once again, I was being abandoned.

Therapy was a terrible experience. Not only were my problems too much for these student therapists, but I knew that I wasn't "normal." Regular, good kids don't have to see therapists. I was sure I had to be pretty fucked up. In fact, I thought I was crazy. Crazy people were the ones who saw therapists, and I was so crazy that the therapists kept leaving without being able to help me. Before

I could warm up to a therapist, even the more talented ones who tried, they moved on. I was even more convinced than ever that no one wanted to be around me. The more anyone tried to help me, the more I felt weird and outcast.

My mother didn't know these therapists weren't right for me. She sent me to the place covered by our insurance. She did what she thought were the right things, but her actions hurt me more than receiving no help at all, and I resented her for it. I built a wall between us. I had been forced into inappropriate therapeutic relationships and onto meds. I believed my mother didn't love me. I imagined that she didn't have my interests in mind because look at what she was doing. I was eleven years old and had words being thrown at me like "mental illness," "bipolar," and "reactive attachment disorder." I didn't know what the hell anyone was talking about. The only thing I knew was that there was something very wrong with me, and I didn't feel like anyone was on my side.

Like everything else in my life, high school started as a disaster. There was a new high school built in Gilroy. I got to go there. They had new procedures too. My mom didn't realize the day we got our schedules was picture day. I remember feeling awful after getting my first high school schedule because I wasn't dressed in the right clothes, and I had a weird feather in my hair for the pictures. It wasn't at all what I would have planned to be memorialized as what I looked like as a freshman. I used that experience as one more reason to fight with my mother.

The violence in our home escalated. I was the instigator of that violence. I had what were euphemistically called "emotional outbursts," during which my parents genuinely feared for their safety. Not knowing what to do with me, they started having me committed to the psych ward.

Commitment is traumatic under the best of circumstances, but for me it was especially so because my parents called the police to have me taken into custody. They did this often. Every incident made me become the four-year-old that first time in the police car after my dad died. Every call to the police made me more violent.

At first, the commitments were short. Sometimes I didn't even have to go to the psych ward. The county where I grew up is odd; they have a thing called Emergency Psych Services (EPS), which is like a holding area. You sit in EPS, and they'll watch you for a period of time, always less than three days. Then they decide from there if you need to go to the psych ward. Since I was a minor, the EPS staff would make this decision with my parents. My mom was always in favor of commitment, pressing for hospitalization. She was having me moved on to become someone else's problem. I didn't understand why I was always being abandoned, unwanted. These feelings led me to a cycle of increasing violence.

The psychiatrists consistently said the same thing. I needed stabilization and revision of my meds, which weren't working at all. I think the medication didn't work because medication doesn't help a person process grief. I still needed to work through my feelings of grief and abandonment, but at that point, I was not willing to participate in therapy. I was overwhelmingly resentful, angry, and sad. I was sick of the revolving door of therapists who couldn't fix me. I wanted to be part of a family I could trust. I was also overweight and had a ton of acne—the normal mixed with the totally abnormal, none of it good.

But I did make one good decision: I stopped being disruptive and started to thrive in class. I liked to learn. I wanted to succeed. I saw that other people were doing well in school. I knew I could too. It was my first positive feeling about myself. I was able to keep my violent outbursts at home.

At the start of senior year, around September, I got into a huge fight with my mom that started off with her asking me to do a chore before I went to a friend's house. I didn't wanna do the chore. I felt like I was being used. I was in this huge story about why she wanted me to work. I ended up coming at her and breaking her phone. The altercation turned violent. Eventually, I picked up a screwdriver and threatened to attack her with it. The police were called. I was brought out in a straitjacket.

Thank God I was still seventeen. I could have ended up in jail or homeless if I had been any older. I spent three weeks highly medicated in a psych ward before a placement in a group home could be found for me. The hospital was terrible, but the group home was worse.

These group homes, called cottages, are in residential areas and look normal enough. In the cottage where I stayed for ten months, there was a living room, a small staff room, a kitchen, two bathrooms, and nine bedrooms. In each bedroom, there were two beds. The rooms were assigned without regard to gender or age. I might have a roommate who was a boy or a girl, anywhere from seven to fifteen years of age. None of us received any help for anything we were going through. We were just being warehoused until the adults in our lives got themselves together or until we were moved deeper into the system. This was a hard situation for an angry seventeen-year-old to deal with, but I managed. I also managed to graduate from high school.

At eighteen, I moved out of my parents' home and started using in earnest. Sure, I'd had a little to drink or some weed when I was younger, but this was different. This was not experimentation. I was using for real. Immediately, everything went to hell.

I had a using buddy who I smoked a lot of weed with. Our lives seemed fine. We both had jobs, and he was gay, so he didn't try to get with me when we were high. Then one night, he told me he had done cocaine. I wanted to do cocaine too! We found a dealer and picked up some cocaine. I used for the first time in a Taco Bell bathroom, and I was hooked straightaway.

My using accelerated from there. It's so gross to look back at those times from sobriety and think about how exciting it seemed. Trust me, doing coke in a fast food restaurant bathroom is not exhilarating in the slightest. It's disgusting, dirty, and low.

After we left Taco Bell that night, I walked around the streets doing everything you wouldn't want your kid to do. I stopped answering my phone. I started blocking numbers. It was a great feeling because it was the biggest "fuck off!" I could think of to my parents. I was going to show them!

Not long after this, I decided to fall in love with a thirty-six-year-old man who worked at a head shop. I was always losing my pipe, so I was constantly at the head shop getting a new one. One night, he invited me over to smoke dabs, which is synthetic marijuana. We ended up having sex, and I passed out at his house. Our relationship started out as a sex thing, but I wanted to be in love with him. I wanted to be in love, period. I told myself we had some crazy spiritual connection. I was attached and extremely codependent.

I moved in with him. He told me he was a violent guy, and I

said that I was a violent girl, so it should work out. Then the first time he was violent with me, he smothered and tried to kill me. I called the police, who arrived quickly. Maybe it was the same police officers who had been carting me off to the psych ward in recent years, but I didn't recognize them because I was high as fuck. At that point, I had been high as fuck for nearly two years.

I remember the police officer asked me, "What do you think someone's trying to do who puts their hands around your neck and puts a pillow over your face?" I didn't say anything. I didn't want to admit that this guy was trying to kill me. I was a classic domestic abuse victim. I didn't want him to go to jail. I didn't want him to be upset with me. I needed him to love me. They took him to jail anyway, thank goodness. I left his apartment and was too afraid to go back.

I moved back in with my parents and started slipping toward a mental breakdown.

In June 2017, I smoked meth and had a psychotic break from it, from stress, and from prolonged untreated mental illness. I started walking around the house naked. I went into my dad's room butt naked, and I told him I was a rapist. My mom called an ambulance when she got home from work.

One more overnight trip to EPS. This time, however, I was an adult. All they did was give me a bus token to get home. I was still in the psychosis and couldn't find the bus route to my house, so I walked the streets, knowing I needed help. I tried to flag down a couple police officers. I went to a gas station and asked the attendant to call the police. I told them I was mentally ill, so they took me back to EPS, but EPS said I couldn't stay because they did not serve homeless drug addicts. No one recognized that I was in a psychotic break. If you think the services for mentally ill children are lacking, there's no help at all for mentally ill adults.

I went home. Instead of the psych ward, I asked to go to rehab. I knew I was a bona fide addict. But my mom was completely fed up. She said that I had to help myself. The problem was, I couldn't.

After a night in the homeless shelter, I walked out, took off all my clothes, and walked down the street naked. I didn't give a fuck that people were looking at me. I kept muttering that I was mentally ill and needed help. The police took me back to EPS. The staff refused to take me. I realized even in the psychosis that I needed to do something to make them help. When they tried to put pants on me, I started kicking as hard as I could. They ended up tranquilizing me, and I was sent once more to a psych ward.

On the ward, I came back to myself a little and finally had the ability to start calling numbers for rehabs. I was flown down to Orange County for detox. It was five days before we realized the facility didn't take my insurance for extended care. They found a rehab place that took my insurance, but I was placed in an outpatient program because I was afraid that residential would be like being in the psych ward, and I didn't want that again.

My sobriety date is August 5, 2017. Very soon, I will be sober for a year.

Rock to Recovery was one of the first groups I attended while being in rehab, and I want to talk about it because Rock to Recovery changed my life. It made me open to what treatment has to offer.

Walking through the door the first time was an amazing experience. I had learned to play music growing up, so seeing the instruments excited me. There was a piano in the room. I was overjoyed! There was creativity in the space. To me, creativity went hand in hand with the acceptance I wanted, and I knew, walking into that room, that I would be accepted.

I was told what Rock to Recovery is, that I was joining a band today. We create music here. We write a song. It sounded fun to me. I remember it was the first time in recovery that I lit up to something. Then we started doing it. The girls started playing, and we wrote lyrics on the board. We wrote a good song. I played the piano. Everyone who worked at the treatment center came in to see what we were doing. I remember seeing the therapist I was going to work with and thinking that she was going to be able to help me. I thought she saw me as a good person. Somehow by creating and playing music, the real me began to emerge.

I didn't play well because I hadn't practiced in so long, but that didn't matter. My playing was good enough. I was finally good enough, and no one judged me. It was a spiritual experience. Rock to Recovery taught me a lot about being less judgmental of myself and others around me. It was a group that accepted me not just as I was but as I could be.

We are improvisational as we write our songs. The process is lighthearted. The lyrics have to do with recovery, so we get uplifted. Recording these songs and playing them back, hearing ourselves, a lot of times there's laughter on the recording. It's pretty frigging funny. We are also taught about what music does for us. It feels like I'm healing my brain.

I'm dual diagnosis, meaning that I have mental illness and addiction. Rock to Recovery helps with both. It uplifts me so that I've been able to handle cravings and irritability better.

I'm not always having my best day in Rock to Recovery. Sometimes I come in, and I don't wanna participate. I don't wanna make music. I don't wanna hear the girl next to me sing. I'm saying, "Fuck this. I'm not doing it." I might be super in ego or angry or whatever. Maybe I'm sad. I'm still accepted, and I get to sit and listen that day. Or I get to sit, and I bang on a drum. Sometimes I bang on a drum not even to the beat. They let me do that. Sometimes I dissociate when I'm in there. Sometimes I'm not comfortable in my skin. It's all OK in that group. I feel safe there. I show up no matter how I feel, which, for me, is quite an accomplishment. A lot of the times, by the end of the session, I'm laughing and smiling with the rest of the group. We're in this thing together.

My life has changed pretty drastically since I got sober. The only person I've talked to during my recovery is my aunt. We talk every Sunday, and she encourages me in my recovery. She is a positive light. She keeps me feeling like I'm connected to my family.

I don't have a relationship with my sister. She's an alcoholic and has lost her child to my adoptive parents. I am afraid she may drink herself to death like our mother did. I haven't talked to my adoptive parents in the better part of a year. They know I'm in treatment and sent me some clothes and stuff, but I said to them that I'm setting a boundary and trying to figure this stuff out. Right now, I need to do that without their interference or input.

My outlook on the future is mixed. I still have this feeling that I have to do something to prove myself to my adoptive family, like a four-year degree or a thriving business, but that isn't realistic, nor do I think it's what they want from me.

I have a lot of work to do on me to change the way I feel about myself, but I practice the twelve steps pretty thoroughly. I see God working actively in my life. I trust in that Higher Power. I often pray about the amends I need to make and how to make them. I have a lot of fear around family. There's so much that still hasn't been addressed. I'm figuring out my part in it and what I need to be responsible for.

What I do know is that I have a purpose. I'm cared for and taken care of. It's possible for me to have relationships with appropriate boundaries. It's possible for me to succeed and grow.

In the future, I see myself going to school and earning some kind of degree or certificate. I am not sure what I'd like to study. I'd like to work in treatment. In the near future, I see myself possibly house managing at a sober living. I see myself getting a second job and making enough money to support myself in an apartment, living with sober roommates. I see myself eventually reconnecting with family and making amends to people I have harmed. Building friendships, relationships, and connections again is my priority.

Remaining sober is a big goal of mine. I really want it. I know there's a promise here that I can have a life if I stay sober. My profession doesn't matter. I'll be OK. I'll be safe. I'll be loved and protected and supported in the twelve step rooms. That's really all I want. I am finally connected to what matters, and I have some confidence that it's not going to be taken away from me.

13

CARYNN

"Spirit Lead Me"
by Michael Ketterer and Influence Music

I think I started getting beat up when I was four years old. My parents had separated before I was born, and they both remarried. My mom married a good man, but he was in the Navy, and he was gone a lot. My biological father married this evil woman who already had two girls, and it was like Cinderella when I had to stay at their house. She was good to her real daughters, but she would abuse me. She hacked at my long hair with scissors and took what was still on my head and dragged me around the house with it, banging me into the walls.

I tried to tell my dad, my mom's husband, but he didn't believe me at first, and like I said, he was gone a lot. I wanted my mom not to know what was happening, so for the longest time, I told her I was playing soccer with the other kids, and I got hurt. But one time, when my dad was there, I came home with my nose broken and a black eye and my teeth chipped. He believed me then. I had to finally admit to my mom what was going on. The two of them got me out of having to go over to my biological father's house. They were totally on my side. And I have to give it to my birth father; after he found out what had been happening, he divorced the bitch.

Though it sounds bad to say it now, I accepted that being abused was part of what I could expect. After my biological father divorced my first stepmother, I found out that abuse didn't have to be physical. It could be other stuff. When the bitch was gone, I could go back over to my birth father's place, and nobody hit me, but he was always insulting my mom, saying terrible things about her. That hurt me too because I knew my mom loved me. He kept saying that she was wrong about everything, denigrating her. I was just a kid, so I felt like her loving me was a big mistake. If she was wrong about everything, she had to be wrong about loving me. I loved her so much. I still do. She's my superhero, so I continued crying and not letting people know.

At school, I got into playing soccer and running and other sports. I was really sorry I used soccer as the lie I told my mom for why I had those injuries because I loved that game. My team in high school won the state cup a whole bunch of times. I was a fast runner, so I also ran track. I was really good at that too. I was getting scouted for a soccer scholarship. I was excited about the chance of going to college. It was like my body was starting to forget it had been abused for so long. But then I really did have a soccer accident and broke my hip. I was in constant pain. I did physical therapy for a year to get back in shape. I couldn't wait to get back to soccer because I still had a chance to go to college.

Just after I was cleared to return to playing, I got rear-ended by a Ford F-350. I was, like, fifteen, and my car was totaled. I got a hairline fracture on my spine and a compressed disc fracture. More pain. The weird thing was that I somehow almost expected it because I was just about always in pain anyway. When I was thirteen, I was diagnosed with endometriosis. My grandmother and mother also had it. The pain from that was really bad and was the reason I started taking Percocet, like they gave my mom. The pills didn't really work great after a while. Still, I knew that there was a way to get rid of pain, physical and emotional. Drugs would do that.

I got into a relationship with a guy when I was sixteen. He was not a good guy, from a pretty bad family except for the three younger kids. The guy had gang ties. He was violent. He would get drunk and beat me up. When I was hurting, his mom told me she was giving me ibuprofen, but I found out later that she was giving me ten-milligram Oxycontins. When I hurt, the pills were kind of like magic, so I wanted them more and more. I was just a kid really, and I didn't know I could get addicted to pills. I just didn't want to hurt, whether it was from endometriosis or getting beat. I was in that relationship for seven years, and I can't say it got any better.

When I was eighteen, he started using heroin. I told myself that I was better than him. I was "only" on pills. But then one day, I really hurt, and I couldn't find any pills, so I tried the heroin. It worked! I didn't hurt.

Then his mom went to jail for drugs, and I became a mom at twenty to her three youngest kids. They were fourteen, eleven, and nine. They had issues of their own: autism, early onset bipolar disorder, and anger issues. I wanted to take care of them. They'd had a horrible home life. I decided to quit using for the first time. I got Suboxone. For a short time, we had a family.

The guy I was involved with went into the Marines to quit,

but when he came back, he started using again. His abusiveness got worse. He would beat me up where the kids couldn't see the bruises. The part I remember so clearly was accepting it. It was so familiar to be beaten like that and have no one care or know. I told myself that living with the pain was normal. I had to deserve it because it was so much a part of my life. I would break off with him, but every time I decided I had to get away, I would take him back because the kids needed me. Of course, like so many abusers, he convinced me that I would never do any better than him. I believed that lie.

I started using again to dull the pain. Still, I wanted to do something good. I wanted to take care of those kids, give them a better life than what they'd had. They were already calling me "Mom." They had become my family. My real family had turned their backs on me because I was a mess when I was on dope. These were the people who needed me.

After one really bad beating, I felt like being abused and taking drugs was all the life I was gonna have if I didn't do something. I called my mom and told her I needed help. She came through for me. She found a treatment facility, the Lighthouse in Orange County, California, a couple of days later. I entered an inpatient program there to get sober. That was when I became part of the Rock to Recovery band. It was so different. I was like, "What is going on?" the first time I participated in the group. The leader was so happy, so cheerful and welcoming. I enjoyed Rock to Recovery and was at the Lighthouse for about two months. When I left, I thought I was sober for good.

My sobriety lasted four months, and then a friend had a medical emergency right in front of me. She lost a baby. There was a lot of blood. After a couple of days, she begged me to show her how to smoke heroin to help her forget what had happened. I thought, "Okay, for *her*, but I'm not gonna get into it myself." Of course, as soon as I started, I binged on it. I was living on the streets, paying a lot for my habit. I lost weight. Soon I was down to about ninety pounds and looked like crap, but I didn't know how bad it was until the guy who sold me the dope told me I really needed help. That got my attention. Mostly your dealer doesn't care how sick you are so long as you are buying. But he saw that I was going to die if I kept at it. Somehow, I listened to him.

The Lighthouse let me come back for another two months. In the beginning, I was too far gone to do much, but slowly I started feeling better. I was ashamed that I had relapsed and gone down so far, so fast. I beat myself up for being such a failure. But when I went back to Rock to Recovery, the same guy was there, smiling at me. I thought he would be disappointed in me, so I edged in against the wall. But he was so glad to see me! He welcomed me and told me he was proud of me for coming back and for still being alive. Nobody had been proud of me for anything since my time playing soccer. And that he was proud of me simply for living— that made an impression.

We immediately went into the making music. I didn't have to think about everything that was wrong, just about the group. Some of them had been in the group when I was there the first time, and they welcomed me too: "Come over here and play the tambourine," or "Do you wanna do the vocals on this one?" The leader played guitar. He was kind and so funny. I had a good time, finding a different way to express myself. I was able to be a version of myself who isn't ashamed or guilty. If I started to feel bad, we put that into the song and flipped it, which made me feel like everything was OK. The whole group would tell me that I'm rad.

Everybody in that room with me was in recovery. We all worked together. Nobody said the things that my abusers told me, that I was a piece of shit. They all believed in me, and that made me start believing in myself too. I was inspired. The group leader told me I was fearless and strong. That made a big difference. For maybe the first time, I really thought I could do something good with my life, not just waste it.

They say in recovery that you can have a life beyond your wildest dreams. As a kid, I always wanted to help people. I felt bad for people who were homeless because I'd been there. I empathized with people struggling with issues I'd struggled with: abusive relationships, pain, addiction, low self-worth. I knew my experience could help them find recovery too.

I've been sober now for two years. I got my family back, plus I have a family in the recovery program that supports me. My family trusts me now. It's almost weird. Before, it was like no one wanted to have anything to do with me, and that's turned around. I have good relationships with my mom and dad. It's like God showed me that I can love people, not judge them, and that means I can try not to judge myself either. I've got my confidence back like I did when I was running and winning. I've got an apartment, I pay bills, and I'm in a good relationship with a boyfriend.

I want a future. I want to get married and get a puppy, and one day I want to open up my own treatment center or someplace where people can go and feel safe so they can recover. I want children. Because of the endometriosis, I may not be able to have any, but adoption is a wonderful possibility. I want to have kids to take care of, to mentor and guide as they grow. But right now, I'm happy with getting a puppy and for not getting beat up anymore. I'm worth more than that, and now I know it.*

*At the time of publication, Carynn is married with a child and a puppy.

ACTIVE-DUTY MILITARY AND VETERANS

Mental Health Issues among Active-Duty Military and Veterans

Veterans with mental health concerns face several issues similar to those seeking treatment for substance abuse, most notably stigma and lack of access to quality care.[19] While it is true that the Veterans' Administration (VA) can be innovative and provide excellent services, accessing those services remains a significant problem for many.[20] Individuals who reside in rural areas don't have access to the same services as those in urban centers, and wait times for the processing of paperwork remain outrageous. These issues can cause many veterans to give up or fall through the cracks, never receiving the care they need, which was promised to them as a benefit of their service.[21] One result of lack of access to quality mental healthcare for veterans has been high suicide rates.[22]

Additionally, active-duty personnel and veterans from all branches of the service often feel shame around mental health issues such as depression or trauma. Whether individuals provided service in combat or noncombat situations, their training includes developing inner and outer strength. Although active-duty military personnel and veterans often share a no-one-left-behind attitude, they also don't want to be the one who needs help. Not only might that be a sign of weakness, which doesn't fit well with the warrior creed, but sometimes individuals seeking help are removed from active duty. Many go untreated, literally hiding from help, to continue to serve.

Furthermore, military training includes ignoring sensation, feelings, weaknesses, and injuries. Individuals are trained to move forward at all costs; the mission must be accomplished. Expressing feelings and describing experiences to civilians without military experience, particularly to their own families, seems impossible to many veterans and active-duty personnel. These feelings of shame and isolation, coupled with lack of access to appropriate care, can lead to emotional breakdown, substance abuse, and suicide.

Our veterans and military personnel deserve a higher level of care than they currently have access to. The cases in this section of the book share the difficulties active-duty personnel and veterans have accessing services, as well as the support and healing that complementary mental health programs like Rock to Recovery provide.

14

MIKE

"Midnight" by August Burns Red

I sat on the edge of my bed with my gun in my hands. I fingered it gently. The weight was familiar. The metal was cool, a coldness that matched my heart. I wanted out. I didn't think I could live with the mistakes I had made, errors that cost others their lives. Was there another option? I believed asking for help would mean an end to my career. Death, of course, was an end to my career too, but somehow that felt more palatable. My family would still be cared for. Suicide was a choice. Discharge took my choices away. I craved care for my family and control of my life, something I didn't feel I had much of.

I am blessed to remain active duty as I heal. I was worried that command would learn how I feel and deem me unfit for duty. That's not the case. They could not be more supportive! If you're hurting, especially if you are a veteran or currently serving, I want you to know that *there is help available to you.* You can come out of the darkness you're in to a better way of life. There are people who love and depend on you. No, it won't be the same life you had before, but it's a good life. So many of us are dying by our own hand. It doesn't have to be that way, not for you. I know. I chose to live.

Even from a young age, I was pretty sure I would go into the military. I come from a military family. My father was a lifer. I thought I knew what service meant. I wanted to live up to the ideal of being part of a second family, of being part of the proverbial "band of brothers."

I was really just a kid when I was deployed the first time, even though I had got married about the time I went into the service. I completed my training and was selected for a special ops assignment. I was a little nonplussed, but I came to be fine with the assignment. It meant I would have responsibility for making sure our people stayed safe, and that was important to me. My desire to keep people safe, particularly our team and my family, is a deeply ingrained value for me. It would take a greater toll than I knew.

I couldn't imagine the stress I would be under until I was actually in combat. I mean I knew there was stress, but it is 24/7 when you are special ops. Everyone is keeping their eyes on you.

I had a critical position. Every action I took, the outcome was my responsibility. Eventually, an error or bad luck would have a bad outcome. It's inevitable.

I found out I could compartmentalize my feelings, stuff them down. Yes, the outcome was my responsibility, but it wouldn't be my fault if it was the mission. I was sure I could handle that. A little word play would make a bad outcome someone else's problem, if only I was perfect. I wanted to do a good job, not just because it was an important job but for my family back home, for my wife and my kids. My family was growing, and I thought about my job as keeping them safe, in addition to keeping the men and women I was overseeing safe. The safety of everyone I cared for rested on my shoulders. I didn't realize until later that I was keeping everybody I was protecting in the same compartment. I knew a lot about the personal dangers of combat; it was the danger to others that got me.

On my sixth deployment, I made my first "mistake." Others don't see it like that. A mistake is an action or judgment that is wrong, "wrong" being the important word. I'm told that a person can do all the right things and still have a bad outcome. That's probably true. Still, I hold myself responsible for this outcome. The results are on me.

I was involved with a major combined operation involving several branches of the military. Elite units. I was in a small aircraft overwatching the men on the ground conducting the actual op. I became focused on a particular area. I got a radio call from the ground force commander telling me they were taking fire from a different building. He wanted me to look closely at what was happening, to guide them out of there. I could see some of our guys had been hit and were down. I relayed the call for the medevac aircraft. Then I concentrated on trying to guide our troops out of there, which was complex because they were carrying the wounded with them.

After our troops left, other forces were going to attack the building where the first shots came from. I could tell there were a lot of civilians in the building; the hostiles like to use them as shields. I didn't realize how many until other forces secured the building. Women and children poured out and only one man.

Our plane was running low of fuel. We cut out to go back to base.

The next day, I found out that a sniper had killed one of our guys. I had stopped looking for danger. I was too focused on one area. I made a mistake.

A guy I was supposed to protect was dead. A guy I had not met but had seen around our small camp. He was twenty-one years old with his whole life ahead of him. I saw his closest friends, a decade younger than me, carrying his casket to the plane home. I was gutted. His death was my fault. I allowed myself to become too narrowly focused, forgot my training and duty. My mistake cost a man his life. I haven't stopped thinking about it since that day.

I started having nightmares every night, so bad that I didn't want to sleep. When I got home, I started drinking in order to sleep. I went on R&R, but before I could spend much time at home or get help for the nightmares, I was deployed again. It was straight back into a combat zone. The nightmares didn't stop.

That was when I started thinking about shooting myself in the head, to stop feeling exhausted and in pain every day. I was unhinged enough that I spent part of each day just thinking of shooting myself. Still, I was eventually selected for command tours.

Once again, I was responsible for the safety of other personnel. Right after I started on this particular deployment, the guys complained that the small planes they were being sent to operations in were being flown unsafely. I reported these complaints to a higher-ranking officer, but he didn't want to hear it. As far as he was concerned, the troops were bellyaching. It was made clear to me that if I was going to fall for complaining, it wouldn't do me any good. I shut up about it. I didn't mention the issues in any of the reports to my leadership. I was having some physical issues by that time too, maybe due to the ongoing tension. I tried to stay focused and busy so I could ignore the nightmares I was still having. Special operators don't gripe. We perform our missions.

I got promoted, awarded a bronze star. Then one of those planes that my folks complained about crashed, killing everyone on board. One of my people was on that plane. I couldn't tune out the feeling that it was my fault, that if I'd insisted on making a report even after my initial concerns had been dismissed, they might all still be alive.

It seemed in my mind that I had made a chart of "people on our side I killed." Each death was like a tick mark on that chart. I had been taking some comfort, deployment after deployment, that I was a protector. I was training the younger guys how to fly overwatch like I did. Now, in my mind, what happened had twisted, so it felt like I only killed the guys I was supposed to protect.

The military kept sending me on tours, and I kept going. I was not spending much time at home. After my ninth deployment, I was so used to feeling horrible that I just went on in a kind of dull haze. I still contemplated killing myself, only the compulsion to pull the trigger was getting stronger.

I'd torn a ligament in my shoulder, and I was trying to ignore that, focusing on work. I received orders for another deployment. Something inside me said, "Enough." I was still dealing with my shoulder issues and had been scheduled for surgery. For the first time, I asked to be let out of the orders. Nine tours were plenty. But my boss said he had to send someone, and if he couldn't send me, he would send my best friend in the unit. I knew that my friend didn't have the training I had, and it could have meant he would be in danger he had not been trained for. I would not have that on my head. I canceled the surgery and went on my tenth tour.

I was the senior officer. I had responsibility for about fifty people. We were to protect civilians from the unfriendlies and train the soldiers in the host nation to do the same. The problem was their social norms were not ours, and they would get handsy or physical with us. We were handicapped in our ability to react because if you responded with force, even if they assaulted you, you got in trouble. The situation was chaotic and frustrating. Somehow, I lasted through the tour, though the nightmares and the suicidal thoughts were getting stronger and stronger.

When I got home, I learned that my eldest child was having some behavioral issues. They were serious. I didn't have the energy to deal with those problems. I didn't have the energy to deal with any problems. My boss told me they were likely going to send me back for a year. I lost hope.

I decided to shoot myself. I sat on the end of my bed after getting my gun. My wife happened to walk in. She knew right away what was going on, how bad off I was. She persuaded me to give her the gun and then begged me to get help. But I believed asking for help would mean the end of my career, and I wouldn't let that happen. By the grace of God, I was not sent back.

I got a job at a different base. I got promoted again. At the party for my promotion, my commanding officer told my wife he could see I had PTSD. He said he would help. In the general's office, I finally broke down, confessed that I thought about shooting myself every damned day and had nightmares every night. He immediately got me the help I need and with dignity! I voluntarily went into a residential treatment program. At that facility, they understood what was going on with me. I began to do better. I finally got a good diagnosis of my physical issues, which identified lung issues that hadn't previously been found, and they got me the right treatment, including surgery for my shoulder. My health in all ways began to improve.

Unfortunately, it took me out of my home, and my son began acting out more. Did improvement in my health have to come at the cost of deterioration in my son's behavior? Again, I judged myself lacking as a protector of my family. I was considered well enough to go home, but my family was deteriorating.

Because of my medical needs, I was offered services for wounded warriors. The AFW2 program also has services for caregivers, which I got my wife into. Through this program, I found Rock to Recovery. I picked up a guitar, and Phil taught me six chords. That was the first thing in years that I unreservedly loved! I bought a nice guitar and started to play regularly.

After returning from the AFW2 event, my son starting acting out violently toward others and himself. I found him after he got violent in his room with his Boy Scout knife. We thought we had removed them all but missed one. My training kicked in, and I got the knife away from him. Where I live, it's the law that you have to call the police after an incident like that. Restraining my son ripped up my shoulder, and my kid had to go into care. It was a difficult time. I called AFW2. They found me support services for him.

I continued my recovery path. I was learning that I had spent years refusing to feel any of my emotions. Every deployment, I had to bottle myself up, and it got harder and harder, so I buried the feelings deeper and deeper in order to keep going. When I played music, I could let myself feel those emotions. In music, I found safety. It was as if the music took me back to who I had been before I ever deployed.

One of the special things about Rock to Recovery's program is that everybody around me was just as battered by darkness and pain as I was, so nobody was judging me. I could go deep into what I felt and have a community to support me as I did. This was the community aspect of the military I had expected to find when I started my career. It was there all along. I learned how to access it.

I led a military-dominated life because it was the life of my choosing. I enjoy being of service to my nation and others. I had grabbed at it when I was young because I thought it was what I was supposed to do with my life. I gave myself the responsibility of being a protector, not realizing that even with my best efforts, I was going to lose people. It's the nature of conflict. Even with our best efforts, we still lose comrades, family, and friends.

I had an image of myself that turned out not to be me at all. It took the music, the songs I wrote, the guys I played beside to show me who I really was back when I was a kid who believed in myself and my dad and the ideal of the military I had as a child.

Playing guitar is a way for me to be mindful and to pray. I needed to be reminded of that connection. I had been just surviving, hanging on. I never reached out the way the music is teaching me I can. Having a connection to something greater than me is helping me let go of that chart of "people on our side I killed." I am learning that I am not all-powerful. That role isn't assigned to me.

I've been playing music with my wife and my kids, and it's helping to heal us as a family, in addition to the way it's working to heal me. I still have nightmares. Just about every night, it feels like I'm sending forces after myself, but I'm not as vulnerable to their poison as I was back before I found what playing guitar could mean to me.

I can't say enough good things about the effects of the Rock to Recovery program on my life. It's given me the tools to help me take my need to be a protector and use it on my family and myself. That's what's important to me right now.

15

HANNAH

"I See You" by Missio

Most people would say I had a pretty boring job. I was a contract specialist with the Air Force. I worked with contracts, pieces of paper with words on them. Not exactly the most dangerous job in the military. I wasn't stationed in combat or in some far-off place where I didn't speak the language or know the customs. I was stateside when I was assaulted by another airman. The attack was brutal. It caused a lot of physical damage and psychological trauma. After multiple surgeries and a post-traumatic stress (PTS) diagnosis, an Air Force medical evaluation board medically retired me.

I was devastated by the forced retirement. I wanted to serve my country. I was in for just under six years before being forced out for no wrongdoing on my part. Now I can't run, can't lift my arms over my head. I am disabled in many ways. I walk with a cane and have a service dog. The life I imagined for myself is gone.

I am part of the Air Force Wounded Warrior program, AFW2. AFW2 exists to provide nonmedical support for combat wounded, injured, or ill airmen and women as we transition into civilian life. There are specific requirements to be part of AFW2. Most people going through a medical evaluation will probably meet those requirements. I'm not entirely sure how I got linked to the program. It might be automatic for anyone undergoing a medical review. AFW2 has been a gift.

Most of what they teach us is resiliency. They share a lot of resources with us. I didn't know all of that when I started with AFW2. I wasn't really paying too much attention because when you're chosen for AFW2, if you're like me, you're really in a very dark place.

It took two years for the medical evaluations to be made in my case. I was in a place of uncertainty that whole time. I'd walk into work every day not knowing if I'd get a letter saying I could return to service, was being kept on active duty, or that I was being retired. The not knowing was unbearable. The stress was constant.

I wasn't introduced to AFW2 until the last two weeks of this process, but the people in the AFW2 program helped alleviate a lot of the things that caused me so much confusion. It was their job to help explain the medical evaluation process to me and get me in touch with the resources I needed to help with my physical and emotional distress.

Each branch of the military has its own division like AFW2. It's DOD (Department of Defense) mandated. AFW2 is the Air Force's program. The Warrior Transition Battalion is what the Army has. Several years ago, shortly after the first wave of people returned from Iraq and Afghanistan, the military found that care for those in transition, especially wounded veterans, was lacking and that people were in substandard positions in terms of how they were living and how they were receiving help. So AFW2 was created to try to catch those airmen in need of support and take care of them during the transition. It's run by the DOD, but it's like its own little division. They have a little bit of the different chain of command, and you can quickly go straight to the top with a problem. Knowing that helps me. I feel heard when I have a concern.

Those two years of not knowing what my status would be with the Air Force were rough. It made my PTS symptoms worse. Once I got with AFW2, the person assigned to me was able to explain to me in two weeks what I hadn't understood for almost the last two years. I was relieved and able to get caught up to speed and figure out what my next steps would be after discharge. AFW2 has been a lifesaver and, really, a game changer for me. It changed how I looked at myself.

Coming to look at the world from a "can do" place was huge for me. Up until that point, I had been told and experienced, "You can't. You can't. You can't." I couldn't remain on active duty. I couldn't maintain my job. I couldn't move the way I wanted. Finally, here were people who were like, "You can, and we're gonna show you how." That started for me with the first program I was involved with in AFW2, the Military Adaptive Sports Program—the Adaptive Sports Camp. I cannot ever be the athlete I was before the assault, but through sports, we are taught that there's always a way around the obstacles we face, no matter what. The sports camp facilitators were able to adapt every sport in a way that I was able to do it. That gave me the ability to look past the "I can't" attitude I had, and I was encouraged to think instead, "All right, so maybe I can't do things the way that I thought I could, but there's still a way."

In the evening, after the sports activities, AFW2 has other forms of resiliency programs. The Air Force brings programs to the camp that help us learn new ways of being, to help us develop toughness instead of giving in to the sadness and grief that come from our changed physical and psychological capacities. Rock to Recovery is one of those programs.

I tried other activities, like comedy and art, but I grew up with music, and I felt like for the longest time, my song had been lost. I play five or six instruments. I hadn't touched any of them in years because I felt like that part of me was dead.

I come from a musical family. My parents met in choir in college. Our family, in a certain way, started from the love of song. But with the assault and the damage to my body, that part of me was lifeless. I didn't whistle or hum anymore. I'd drive down the road, and I wouldn't even play the radio. I lived in silence. It was a very dark time. The truth is, like so many other veterans, I wanted to die. I saw no point to living a life as limited and bleak as mine had become.

Rock to Recovery is very different from other musical programs I have taken part in. We are encouraged to play and sing, sure, but we are also encouraged to write the lyrics to our own songs. Wes and the team come in, and they help us create a song that's entirely our own. They helped me give a voice to a story that's really hard to tell, a story I didn't have another way to share. I think that that's important because they're the first step in being able to talk about recovering your song in a beautiful way.

At my first CARE event with AFW2, I was really nervous and having a hard time expressing myself in acceptable and appropriate ways. The truth was I was so bitter and angry, I had no hope left in life. This event was my last resort. I was suicidal, and in my grief and anger, I lashed out at everyone around me.

Wes seemed unaffected by my anger. He encouraged me to express what I was experiencing in song. I didn't feel like I had the words. Rock to Recovery taught me that's OK. Being with others who were experiencing the same thing, similar things, and totally different things was enough to help me start on that path of self-expression. Wes and his team are able to take on anyone at any level and get them involved and engaged. I sat beside someone who had never played an instrument in his life, yet by the end of the night, each of us, regardless of skill level or initial interest, was holding an instrument and playing a song. Not only were we playing, but we were a community. Together we were stronger, creating music as one and drawing comfort from and building each other up. The music was important, but the community we built was greater than the song.

Wes inspired me to find my words. I went back to my room that night and cried. I seemed like a hard and angry person, but I was really hurt. Before the end of the week, words poured out of me. I wrote a poem about my desire to die. I shared it with Wes and the rest of the band. Instead of telling me I was wrong or that I shouldn't feel that way, Wes instead asked me to share my truth and sing it as a spoken word piece. He incorporated my poem into our song, and I stood in front of an airplane hangar full of people and sang my truth—that so much had been taken from me that I wanted to die. They didn't turn their backs on me. My piece was met with applause, and I learned I wasn't the only person in the room who had felt like that. In that knowing, something shifted inside me. I believed that change was possible.

My recovery hasn't been a clean shot in one direction. I have had setbacks. One of the things that did a number on me was the loss of Bobby Connelly. He was a traveling first sergeant. He loved music too; I mean he really loved music. He loved Wes and the Rock to Recovery team. When he first got involved in our program, Rock to Recovery was one of the biggest things for him. He freaking loved it. He was in his element. Then just like that, he was gone. He passed away last year very suddenly, right after one of our camps.

My last memory of him is singing with him in Rock to Recovery, which is a beautiful memory but also something that's been really hard to process. I pulled away from Rock to Recovery a little after Bobby's death. But I knew Bobby wouldn't want that for me. Wes let me pull away and then made room for me to return. Once more, I can express through song my sorrow, and love, and that shared friendship in the brotherhood that all of us go through.

We veterans in the AFW2 program, so many of us are experiencing the same kinds of things—maybe not the same things specifically but the same kinds of emotions and obstacles we have to overcome... well, *get* to overcome, because some people don't make it. Some people choose a different way out. I don't want that anymore. To be able to write a song that has an impact on everyone who hears it, with words, just words of hope and encouragement, it's really big.

That's one of the important things about Rock to Recovery. Wes and the team let us share our darkness, but they don't let us stay there. All our songs circle around and find an element of hope. That's the chorus: the joy of living, and the possibility, and the hope.

I think being so connected to someone who loved the program as much as Bobby did has helped me overcome some of my pain and anger at being assaulted by another airman. I don't feel alone anymore. That's a gift of both Rock to Recovery and AFW2, the sense that I'm not battling it all alone any longer. I have support and encouragement. Not everyone is ugly or cruel. Yes, we encounter brutal, mean, vicious people, but for the most part, I think everybody's just trying to get through life without trying to mess it up for everybody else.

Think about it like this. We're all walking through a crowded room trying not to bump into anybody. Now I've found myself in a room full of people where we're asked to say, "You're rad." At first, I thought that was silly, but now I am able to see more and more good in people. It's a beautiful thing to be able to love people again. Being brutally assaulted by another airman made me bitter. I withheld myself. I was angry. I had become outwardly hostile and inwardly suicidal when I started with AFW2 and Rock to Recovery. But the music has helped me express and work out those feelings of anger and resentment, and I was able to make room for more love and joy and empathy toward other people.

One of my favorite parts of Rock to Recovery is the connection. The first time we met, for the first two hours, we didn't do anything musically. Wes put us all in a circle. We shared our names and a little bit about ourselves. This sharing time created an environment where, right off the bat, before we'd even touched an instrument, we were a family. Wes made us a group.

We all understand that every single one of us has been going through something. Each of us has something to express. Wes often asks what we want to get out of this session and what is something we wanna let go of. I think that that's beautiful because there have been many times when I've come into the room, and I haven't been in the right mindset. He'll say something that changes what I'm feeling into something more positive and hopeful.

I realized that what I wanted was to know joy or peace. I wanted, like many others in the room, to let go of the negativity I'd been stuck in. That's when we bring in the music, after we set this intention for letting something new into our lives. It's more than banging on a couple of drums. It's a healing process that I can't really describe. We heal through connection before we even touch an instrument.

Another powerful aspect of Rock to Recovery that speaks to me is that everybody involved as a facilitator is at a place in their lives where they can help others look toward enlightenment and healing. They can help us look toward peace and joy because they've been through the shit too. Wes' story is full of defeat and challenges. He has been through that grind too, and that's what it's all about. He can say, "No, I haven't had your exact experience, but I can tell you that there is recovery and hope, and if you play, if you come in this direction with me, you're going to find love." Rock to Recovery points us all in the direction of love.

Rock to Recovery has given me courage. I had the honor of participating in the Invictus Games in 2019 in Australia, and I now teach painting with AFW2. Often, I can hear the music and feel the beat from the Rock to Recovery room floating down the hall. I always stop by to say hi because I will never forget the way Rock to Recovery helped spark the transformation in my heart and gave me back my song.

Hannah now identifies as nonbinary and has changed their name to Hanley.

Sunday

By Hannah (Hanley)

I almost shot myself on Sunday,
The darkness closing in.
They said, "Chill out, man, it's a fun day,
Just take your car out for a spin."
If I can make it to Monday,
I can let the week begin.
Cancel plans for Tuesday,
Much to my chagrin.
Pull myself through Wednesday,
Eating veggies from a tin.
'Cause I won't make it to market Thursday,
I jump at the drop of a pin.
I won't go out on Friday,
But I will stay home and binge.
If I can just breathe through Saturday,
I'll call it a win.
I almost shot myself on Sunday,
Here we go again.
Here I go again.
Here I go.

16

PASTOR

"Power to Love" by Jimi Hendrix

My whole life, I had three things I could always depend on, two real good and one pretty bad. The good ones were what got me through the bad one, and they're still doing it. The good ones are music and God. The bad one is racism.

I was born in Mississippi, and even as a little kid—we left and came to California when I was six—I knew that being black in the South in the '50s wasn't real good. My mother had her life threatened when my father was away, and we had to work in the cotton fields to get money to live. I was the oldest kid, so I was working in the field with my mom. I couldn't do all that much. I was just little, but she needed help. I was always afraid, so I was really glad when my father brought my brothers and me out to be with him. I was glad to get away from the hatred and the threats.

California was better. We didn't have to be scared all the time. My father was living in Ventura, in a place called Tortilla Flats, and we liked it a lot. There were blacks like us, Hispanics, whites, and Asians, all together. Everybody knew one another, and we looked out for one another and got along. I wish we could've stayed there, but our community was where they picked to build the 101 freeway in that area, and they made us move out. We couldn't all go to the same place, so we had to scatter.

Where my family moved to, there was a church right across the street, a Pentecostal church. We didn't go there. My father was a minister, and he had his own church, the Church of God and Christ, and I used to go all the time with him.

The first good thing, the most important that I can depend on, is God. I was raised up in a Christian home, going to church every week, so when I became a minister like my father, I served the Church of God and Christ. But that was later. It was enough that my father made sure I knew God would always be there for me, always watch out for me. He believed that I would have a good life, and for a while when I was growing up, I took that for gospel. He was a man of great faith, and I was easily convinced that he had to be right.

I graduated from Ventura High School and started college, but it was 1970, and the war in 'Nam was going on. They had the draft on then, and some of the guys I grew up with were going over, but they weren't in college. I thought I'd be OK because there were these deferments you got if you were in school. They didn't make you join up.

Only it turned out that the white guys got the deferments, and guys like me got draft notices. There were always reasons we couldn't play the deferment card. Another black guy, one of my buddies, had the same thing happen to him, so we talked about it and decided we would join the Marines together rather than go into the Army. I don't know what his reason for picking the

Marines was. I liked the uniforms. But my buddy failed the physical, so he didn't have to go at all. Meanwhile, I was singled out by the drill sergeant. I was the one he spent time yelling at and making me look bad, sort of hazed me. That first night in boot camp, I lay in my bunk, and I wondered what I'd got myself in for without a friend. I was saying to myself that I was going to die alone. It was a tough time, but I got through it.

Before I was anywhere near ready, I was on deployment and carrying a weapon. I didn't want to shoot anybody, let alone kill someone. At the beginning, when we had to do a patrol, I'd make sure I was in the back, not just because I thought the ones up front would have to do most of the shooting but because when I had to fire my rifle, I pointed it up at an angle so that there wouldn't be any chance of my hitting anyone. Luckily, after a while, I got assigned to a special weapons platoon. We had a major weapon, but a couple of the other guys fired it, and the rest of us were just there to guard them. I don't know how long I'd have been there, but I really didn't want to be in a war. I wanted to be back in the States with my buddies and no killing.

But there was one thing about being in country: it really kicked up my praying. I prayed all the time that I wouldn't have to kill anyone and that I'd get to go home alive. I started to feel like I was really being listened to. Then something happened so that I knew God was protecting me. It was one of those clear signs so that if you have any doubts, they're just blown away. There was a day when I was walking a perimeter by myself, and suddenly the enemy came out of the jungle. I froze, but it was like they didn't see me. I mean I was sure they were looking right at me, but there was no reaction, like I was invisible. I walked right past them in the open. That was my signal that God had His hands on my life, just like my father always told me.

God brought me home, but things don't always happen the way you imagine they will. I got rotated out, and that ended my deployment and got me sent to Camp Pendleton. Once I was home, I was thinking of signing up for another hitch, but I had a girlfriend who was a nurse, and she got pregnant. I got discharged.

I went to work at Community Memorial Hospital in Ventura. My girlfriend knew some of the doctors there, pulled some strings, and got me work, and then I could go back to college. I worked at the hospital and specialized in hematology. I was working in laboratories for about three years, and I had a family and kids. I was really happy with my life those years because I was doing things that helped other people. I got to be of service to others and to make the world a kinder place. I would've done that for lots of years more, but my back went bad.

I was diagnosed with spinal stenosis. I had to stop working at the hospital. It was kind of like God was telling me it was time to move to a different way of serving Him and everybody else. Giving up the job wasn't what was most distressing for me. What hurt my soul was that I had to give up playing the guitar.

Music, my guitars—I had a bass guitar, six-string, and twelve-string—I played rock-and-roll! Standing up and jiving, playing praise music in church, that was the third thing that was a constant in my life. That was one of the things that brought me joy. I played in my father's church, and when he died in 1993, I kind of unofficially took over the church for him until the stenosis made it impossible for me to keep playing.

Then the church got rented out, and I went to Bible college.

I needed to stay really close to God when I lost the ability to pray through my music. I always believed that God had a plan for me, and I didn't know what it was in advance, but I was willing to live by that plan. I just hoped that I could get my music back because it was such a part of the way I prayed.

For a couple of years, I was going in and out of hospitals because of my back and the stuff it was doing to my body, but I kept up the good work, studying and helping people, until in about 2000, when I felt a strong call to active ministry. I'd been serving God by going into jails and suchlike, bringing Christ to people who needed to know that there was a way to hope and that I could offer them the best way I found to change my life so it could change theirs too. But it was all kind of like not enough, until I thought that I should become an official minister. In 2000, I was ordained by the bishop of the Church of God and Christ, and I went and opened my own church and ministered to the people who came.

More and more started coming, and I kept sort of working through the pain and weakness of being ill. I was really physically weak, and doing all the good work was what I wanted, but my spine was degenerating, and I was the person in the church who had to do everything, like setting up and all. By 2017, I had to go to the VA to try to get treatment.

The worst part of the stenosis was that it made my hands stop working because it cut off the nerves to my arms. Then the nerve cutoff started spreading, and for a while, I was paralyzed because my legs stopped working too. For two months, I was just lying there praying to be able to keep doing my ministry, and in the back of my mind, I was hoping somehow to get my music back. It was such a big part of my prayers, and I wanted to praise God to the very most I could manage. I stayed as upbeat as I could because I knew God would want me to.

The doctors finally did the surgery I needed. After that, I started to get some feeling back. It was very slow, but I kept feeling that God was taking care of me. He knew what was best for me. I never thought that He was testing my faith because He had always had His hands on my life. Even though I was not able to do everything I used to, I thought that some movement would always come back. I just didn't know how, and I had to keep telling myself that in case it didn't all come back, I would still find a way to serve God and other people. I had faith that God would show me what I was supposed to do.

After the surgery, they sent me to rehab for therapy. One of the programs in the rehab was Rock to Recovery. Well, I saw the word "rock," and I saw that it was about music, and I went right in. I told them I was a guitarist, but I hadn't been able to play for a while because of my hands. The leader says, "OK, right now you're going to sing." And I said, "I came in to try to play the guitar again," but I'm thinking, "If I'm supposed to sing now, OK. God, thanks for telling me." The leader brings the mic over to me, and he sets me up with these other guys, one playing the organ and another the drums and some on tambourines and other simple instruments. Then he picks up a pencil and a pad and asks us to say how we're feeling. I answer that I'm happy to be where there's music. He gives me the pad and pencil and says, "You write this down."

Now, not only can't I play the guitar, but because my hands don't work right, I can't write very good. But I do it, and we keep going from there. I'm realizing that I got brought here because God knew it was what I needed to start getting back to being able to use my hands again. I got brought to where I needed to be so that people could help me. By being there, I could help the other guys, too, because of my spiritual background, my worship and praise. I always wanted to help others, not myself, and there I was. When they heard me singing, it encouraged them to play or sing, and they were enjoying that. I was helping again! When I saw that, it touched my heart. I knew I was getting blessed because God knew what I needed and that it would be easier for me to get help if I was helping.

I always knew I was blessed, and I always wanted to show other people that they could get blessings too. I know that was God's plan for me all along.

17

ROBERT

"Danger Zone" by Kenny Loggins

My road to the Air Force Wounded Warrior (AFW2) program started when I was a combat rescue helicopter pilot. I always wanted to fly helicopters because I thought it was just so much fun. I started out more as an adrenaline junkie than anything else. That put me on my path to trauma.

I was in Afghanistan in 2010 doing combat rescue, most of it on medevac missions. That's medical evacuation, like what an ambulance driver does in the States. During those months I was deployed, my crew did 221 missions. We carried EMTs who seamlessly integrate with every other special ops team that we have in country, in a lot of situations with SEALs and Delta and different Army units. I considered myself just an ambulance driver.

If they called us to scramble, you sprinted, got in the aircraft, and you'd go. You find out during that process where you're going. It doesn't matter if the people you need to pick up are still taking fire or if they're in the middle of a minefield; you have to sort it out.

That sort of thing didn't bother me, but I wasn't prepared for the number of patients that we had, or for the severity of the injuries, or the children. I kind of assumed the injured would be mostly allied troops, soldiers, airmen, sailors, that type of thing, but it was a lot of civilians, a lot of innocents. I struggled with that. When it happens, it's overwhelming, and it's huge the amount of stress, energy, and trauma that a person can carry with them after that situation. I was getting really angry, but I didn't want to deal with what was causing the anger.

There was a huge troop surge, and I arrived there as one of the guys working casualty evaluation. I went in without addiction issues. I enjoyed beer and liquor, and I could get crazy and whatnot at times, but I knew how to have control and responsibility with it. When I got home, I had none. If I didn't have a drink, I started feeling anxious and pissed off. I didn't realize I completely was overtaken by post-traumatic stress disorder (PTSD).

I used substances to self-medicate. Not severely at first, but as time went on, I got worse and worse. Within a few years, I was a full-blown alcoholic. There were a lot of other impulsive behaviors I was doing. At first, I just considered it a problem with alcohol. I didn't consider PTSD. Then I began to have other addictions: sex, porn, sugar, and exercise, which was still part of my addiction to adrenaline.

I had numerous sports injuries, and once I got into a really bad motorcycle accident. I didn't realize that my reckless behavior was a kind of suicide wish. I thought everything that was wrong was somebody else's fault. A person with PTSD wants to point the finger away from themselves. After I started finding out about PTSD,

I split up with my ex. We had two kids, and I—with my anxiety and whatnot—seriously thought the split was because she was being a controlling bitch about everything.

When I had the motorcycle accident, I lost my pilot qualification because I added a brain injury to the PTSD during the accident. I did everything in my power to fly again, without looking at how badly I was messing myself up. My life just kept going downhill. I was just trying to keep my job and cover up my problems. I was still a captain in the military. I had been selected for promotion to major, but it all spiraled way out of control. I did a tour in Africa in the middle of all this, trying to keep my job. I was deployable again, but I wasn't allowed to fly.

The military isn't equipped to handle people like me. I needed to get a medical waiver, but they're so backed up with so many years of war and so many people that are waiting on these waivers that it took a few weeks shy of two years. In the meantime, I switched to drones for two months, and all I can say about that is that we killed 2.1 people per day in the horn of Africa.

I continued trying to cope privately with the PTSD, and that exacerbated it through the roof. The addictions to help me live with it went up exponentially too. Inside, I was ashamed, but I was not admitting anything. What I would do is bounce from one addiction to the next, whether it was sex or porn or alcohol—anything I could get legally. I wasn't asking for help. That's a hallmark of PTSD, especially among military personnel. You don't trust anybody to help you. And, quite honestly, I don't think the military knows what to do with people in that situation.

I only did the drones for a couple months, and then I was stationed stateside. I came home from Africa in the spring of '13.

That was when I came clean to my wife. I just collapsed onto her and told her almost everything. I told her I needed to get out of that job. It was killing me. But I couldn't be a normal husband with her or a normal father for my kids, and I blamed them for that. In the eighteen months it took to go through the medical board—that's how backed up they were—I got less and less easy to be close to. I didn't want to be around people. I didn't get out of the military until October 2015.

During that time, I blew out my knee. Medical care was on base, but all the doctors were deployed. It was just the med technician sewing me up. I got staph bacteria in the joint. They kept me in the base hospital, and that gave me access to unlimited opiates. I developed an opiate addiction. You know, if you start mixing opioids, sleep aids, and benzos, you've got a cocktail for overdose. I was mixing all that stuff. I didn't care. I quit alcohol. I had actually gone to a detox for two days in Vegas (that's where I was stationed), so quitting drinking cold turkey was no problem because I had all these other addictive substances around me. The staph meant I had to have a number of surgeries, and all the while the military was messing with me about medical retirement.

One of the things they did was to say I was getting a medical discharge for noncombat reasons. That made me crazy! How could they not see that the start of my problems came from combat, from pulling kids out of horrific situations? You have no idea what people will do to children in a war. I was in a really depressed, dark place.

That's when I drifted into passive suicide. Within two to three months, it started becoming deliberate. One of my most common coping things was as soon as I felt anxiety, I didn't want to have an embarrassing outburst, so I would leave. It didn't matter where I was. If I was in a car, it didn't matter. It didn't matter if the car was on the interstate. I don't even know how many times I jumped out of cars.

Then I made a genuine attempt. This is what caused me to change. I went to my gun safe, grabbed my pistol, picked it up, put it to my head, and pulled the trigger. There was nothing in it. I have no idea who unloaded it. I put in a loaded magazine and hit the slide release; the round jammed going in. That seemed to be the universe telling me to live.

I wasn't sure how I was going to do that yet. The military wasn't giving me any help, and my wife had divorced me. My isolation just got deeper. I think that's true of other guys with PTSD too. After the suicide attempt, I was able to look at a lot of the painful memories and see them without letting them destroy me. I could see it from an outside perspective and not look at that and go, "Oh, my ex is a bitch. It was her fault that we split up." No, I was really freaked out from my kids running around upstairs. The noise freaked me out, and I blamed my anxiety on that woman. I was still having problems living with all the horrible injuries I'd seen on deployment or the people we killed with the drones. I started to recognize what those memories had done to me.

Any memory from that point on, my perspective of my whole life basically changed. I no longer wanted to kill myself. I knew exactly what would have happened if I hadn't made that shift. It's happened to so many other vets. I would have killed myself. If this shift hadn't occurred, I'd be dead.

I met the wife I have now, and we got married. I was working on having a good relationship again. I was medically retired, and I became, instantaneously, a conscientious objector. I was able to see where and how I bought into everything, how I had been brought from a pilot who rescued people to a man who killed.

A night or two before my suicide attempt, my wife and I were talking about staying in Vegas. We had found our "retirement home," even though we were both young, or relatively young for that, and she was doing really well in real estate. I was gonna be helping her with that. We had a real good business plan set up. But when I had the experience with the jammed gun, I told her, "I can't stand Vegas." She asked, "What do you want to do?" I had two kids with my ex who are out in Denver, and I said, "I think I've got to go to Colorado." Without hesitation, my wife said, "All right. I'll go with you." She quit her job; we took a leap of faith on the VA, and we didn't tell anybody.

The leap of faith didn't pay off. I wasn't getting paid by the VA. I had no medical coverage. I had nothing. I retired as a major, but we weren't paid for four months. I didn't have medical for seven months. They screwed up my education. I couldn't get GI Bill money. It took forever to get vocational rehab. It was just in every single area they screwed up. I was so low and so bitter. My one idea was to start a webpage called Broken Promises and have people who hated the VA and were experiencing this go on and post crap about them. I wanted to provide a forum for people like me. We might not be able to improve the system, but we could complain loudly.

Then I had a friend email me about the Air Force Wounded Warrior program. Mostly, I didn't talk to people because I was so miserable. I wrote back to him saying, "What the hell is this? I'm not going." AFW2 is a military program, and the military wasn't giving me shit. Then he called me on the phone. If I hadn't known him as well as I did, I wouldn't have answered, but I respected him. We were actually in a motorcycle club together back when I was doing really reckless and dangerous things.

He talked me into the weeklong camp. I couldn't believe it. When he called, things were really bad. I still had a real bad staph infection in my knee. There were three holes that oozed daily. Against all odds, I had to do my own knee surgery because the VA wouldn't. The VA told me to go to the ER. The ER doesn't do orthopedic surgeries. They advised me that I needed to get into surgery right away. If I didn't, I was facing amputation or death. So I found myself in the bathroom, spraying hydrogen peroxide on my knee and digging down into some of the holes, pulling out infected tissue. That's the situation the VA left me in. I have to say that it gave me confidence that I could get past anything, but I sure don't recommend it.

The camp was just a few weeks later. That's when I hooked up with Rock to Recovery. Doing music with other people was something I'd never done before. I didn't even know how to believe in myself. But I thought, "Oh, screw it. Let me try this."

The first night, we created one song, and we created one song the second night. I knew how to pick at the strings a little bit on the guitar, but it doesn't really matter whether you can play or not. The coolest thing was that writing these songs gave me something to do. I was able to walk a little, and that was it. It was difficult getting in and out of cars. I couldn't go out hiking or biking. My activities were limited.

I had had such bad PTSD I hardly ever left the house. Rock to Recovery gave me something to do every day. I can't tell you how big that was. When I got home from that week, that first night home, it was a complete, complete hallelujah, spiritual awakening experience. It was, "Oh my God, I really can trust people again." It was, "I do need others." Not only that, I knew that when I got healthy, I could help other people too. That night, for me, was a huge change. I said to myself, "Holy shit. I can have a *life* again. I've got a purpose. I can do something. I know exactly what I want to do."

Getting back and working to help other people with their lives, making them better or whatever, was a big deal. It became a driving factor for me. I see too many news stories about vets committing suicide and occasionally stories such as "Two-star general commits suicide." The stories usually say something like, "No one knew he had this…"

I want to help because I can see what others refuse to see. Yes, I'm an Air Force Academy graduate, pilot, officer. I've got all the boxes checked in regard to respectfulness for our society. Then I come home from Afghanistan and nearly instantly get rid of my wife and kids. Within two or three months, they were gone. I would cuss my ex out if she'd send me pictures of my kids in a text message. I tried the bad coping strategies. I did the "I don't care if I live or die" behavior. Drinking and driving. Beyond crazy use of pills. Jumping out of cars. Putting a gun to my head. I want to say this again because it's happening to so many people. Their families see it. PTSD makes them just look down on themselves. They point the finger at themselves, and then they clam up. A lot of vets are stuck in that sort of lifestyle. The military either isn't able or equipped to help the way it should. Programs like Rock to Recovery help.

I've been involved with the Rock to Recovery program for about a year and a half. One of the things that keeps me engaged is that the music ties experiences to emotions that I can't get to otherwise. I use music to give me a way to look at and begin to deal with those emotions. When I'm doing the music, I fully get into it and immerse myself into it. I can't deny who I am any longer. That's the most powerful thing about what Rock to Recovery does. It forces me to go through that emotional experience and supports me in the reflection and self-examination that come after. It gives me the ability to start answering some of those "why" questions that I wouldn't even admit to having before. I am no longer trapped or fearful of the answers.

Without music helping me look at myself, I don't know that I ever would have improved much or been willing to talk about my addictions or my recklessness. Shame causes people to clam shut. I had no idea how damaging the activities I was doing were to the people in my life—to my ex and my kids. I didn't see how impulsive I was and how that hurt them. Once I saw how my behavior caused harm, I shut down. Now I know that's actually the wrong thing. Seeing the behavior, that's the time to get help so that it can change. PTSD is a problem that can be overcome.

My trauma destroyed my first marriage and almost destroyed me, but I'm a different person for my family now. Back then, if my kids wanted to be around Dad, he was always in the other room. Now I want to be there for them. My wife and I have started a home business. I went to a nonprofit farming school called Veterans to Farmers that I got into last summer. My wife is starting off with essential oils. The plan is to eventually open up a holistic-style healing ranch. We're both doing music for fun. We practice music daily or listen to it with the kids. We do dance parties with them a lot.

The trauma is still there, but it's lost the strength to destroy me. If you have struggles like mine, I want to say, "Hey, this is how others helped me, and, by the way, I hope we can help you. You're not alone."

THE RESEARCHER

Music and the Brain

Humans have known for thousands of years that music has a therapeutic effect on body, mind, and spirit. Modern research tools, particularly those used to study the brain, have been developed to measure that therapeutic effect. The field that studies the impact of music on the brain is called neuromusicology.[23]

Clinicians use music in different types of treatment situations to improve outcomes. From a behavioral health perspective, it is not only neurological repair that can play a role in helping to heal addiction, depression, trauma, and other issues, but it is also the emotional response people have to music. Emotion and mood are affected by music, which can have a profound effect on the willingness and ability of individuals to meet short-term treatment goals like staying or actively engaging in treatment.

Comparing the Brains of Musicians and Non-Musicians

Scans that compare the brains of professional musicians to those of non-musicians show interesting results. Professional musicians tend to have brains that are bigger, more sensitive, and better connected than non-musicians.[24] Parts of musicians' brains that are larger than average include the corpus callosum and the areas responsible for motor control, coordination, and auditory processing. The larger size of the corpus callosum indicates that musicians' brains communicate more effectively between the two hemispheres than non-musicians.' Musicians' brains are more symmetrical than those of non-musicians, brain symmetry being related to overall brain health. Musicians also tend to have better auditory skills, memory, and cognitive ability than non-musicians.[25]

Rewiring the Brain

The good news for those who are not musicians is that our brains are neuroplastic; they are able to change and develop in response to stimulation.[26] As we go through life, we fire up different parts of the brain. Connections get stronger the more they are fired. There is a saying in neurology that "what fires together wires together." Musicians' brains grow because they are constantly firing various parts of the brain by engaging in ongoing music practice. Compare this to those who suffer from addiction. Addicts develop a different neurology, which becomes neuropathology, by constantly drug seeking and engaging in substance misuse. By understanding how the brain wires and rewires itself, we can use that information in treatment to help the brain rewire itself in healthier and more productive ways.

The evidence is clear: playing music and singing stimulates and activates almost every part of the brain. When people say that music has touched or moved them, they are expressing a very real experience. Tonal vibrations affect the body and mind in ways that we are still coming to understand. What is known is that because the brain is so active while listening to music, music can in a sense jolt the brain out of set patterns, if only temporarily at first. This can have a profound impact in addiction or trauma treatment.

When someone in treatment for addiction or trauma comes into a Rock to Recovery session, their mind is engaged in obsessive thoughts. Both addiction and trauma are characterized by excessive thought patterns: fixations on using drugs or reliving a past experience. But music, because of the way it engages the brain, breaks through that obsessive pattern and allows for a different experience. The individual, through music, experiences relief from compulsivity and at the same time the joy and pride of creative expression. Over time, by repeatedly breaking the obsessive thought pattern, the brain is able to rewire itself in different, healthier directions.

Brain Chemistry

One of the ways in which music affects mood is that it causes the formation of important brain chemicals. Neurotransmitters are chemicals that diffuse across synapses, allowing neurons in the brain to communicate with one another. Music increases the production of dopamine, an important neurotransmitter that is part of the pleasure and reward system. This is the feel-good chemical responsible for the pleasure of orgasm and eating chocolate. Dopamine levels can increase by as much as 9 percent among people who are listening to music they enjoy.[27] Serotonin, another feel-good chemical and neurotransmitter, is also released when individuals play music.[28]

Endorphins are hormones secreted in the brain that make a person feel good. They are known to activate the opiate receptors in the brain and are important for the reduction of both physical and emotional pain. The hormone oxytocin,[29] which helps individuals bond with or trust one another, is also secreted when people play music together or listen to live music. There is even new research that indicates the playing of music and music-based cognitive therapies likely have regenerative qualities within the brain.

Emotional Upliftment

Positive or uplifting lyrics also have an impact on the brain and mood. They create prosocial behavior, the tendency to take actions that help and support others.[30] This can come in the form of prosocial emotions, like empathy or kindness, or actions like cooperation and generosity. These impacts are amplified when individuals come together to create music. When prosocial feelings are combined with lyrics that promote mutual aid, support, and kindness, the group begins to act toward creating those outcomes. These actions will last well past the music session and can be reignited by remembering the session or listening to the song created.

One way to respond to the crises of addiction, trauma, suicidal ideation, and a host of other mental health issues is to provide interventions and therapies that allow individuals to express their feelings in a situation where there is safety and no judgment. There are many types of activities that do this. One is Rock to Recovery.

The final story belongs to Doc, Rock to Recovery's vice president, who stumbled into a session one day and fell in love with what we do.

18

CONSTANCE SCHARFF, PHD

"Do You Feel Loved" by U2

I used to believe that the only thing that kept me alive was my ability not to feel anything. If I felt what I was going through, my only option would have been suicide; at least, that was true when I was a little girl.

My story truly begins just before my seventh birthday. It was Saturday, and I was lying in bed with my father, watching cartoons. My mother and brother had driven to town to pick up a birthday cake for me. We lived far out in the country on a farm in California's central valley. The drive to town was considerable. I had no idea what kind of cake my mother was going to bring home. I had asked for chocolate with cherries. I loved cherries.

As I waited in anticipation of their return, my father stroked my hair. I leaned against his enormous belly. I was getting big enough that I could not hide entirely behind his belly. I had always liked hiding on one side of his stomach while my little brother hid on the other. Then we'd pop up on either side like a living jack-in-the-box. I think it irritated my father, but he tolerated it. That day, though, it was just the two of us. I felt safe. I couldn't have been more wrong.

Without warning, my dad slid his hand from my head to the small of my back. He laid me down. I didn't fight him. He was probably close to 350 pounds and mean. I knew that if I fought him, he'd likely kill me. When he climbed on top of me, I wanted to scream, but I couldn't breathe. His bulk crushed the air out of me.

I remember only the first seconds of the rape, the moment of penetration. The sensation was unreal, a searing pain tearing me apart. I couldn't take it—the pain, the betrayal, the horror—and so I left my body. I was gone. My spirit floated away to watch the dead-looking little girl in the bed from a tree in the garden. That was my first dissociative experience. I have only a few foggy memories of the next three years. I learned how not to be present. The pain of living with that kind of abuse was more than a little girl could bear.

When I started drinking, I wanted that same numbness. I was eleven when I had my first drink. My parents had divorced, and I moved with my mother and brother to a rusted-out, single-wide trailer in rural Oregon. Living far from my father, some of the trauma nested inside me began to surface. I innately knew that drinking would keep the feelings at bay.

I was in the barn doing my chores when, without reason or warning, I put away the horse apple fork and made my way up to the house. In a cabinet above the fridge, my mom stored a few bottles of liquor for guests. I got a chair from the kitchen table and pulled the bottles carefully down. At the sink, I poured about an ounce from each one, filling a tall glass. After I put the bottles away, I stood over the sink, pinching my nose, and drank the entire concoction. The taste was vile, but the effect was immediate. I was drunk. I rinsed out the glass and went back to the barn, where I lay in the hay as the world spun. I felt nothing at all. I wanted to stay in that numbness for the rest of my life.

I think it's important to note that no one in my immediate family drank to excess. My mother's people, at least those around me, didn't drink at all, and my father's family drank only before and with dinner in a social and agreeable manner. My father would sometimes drink Jack but, again, never in a way that seemed to change his behavior. Those bottles I pulled down from the cabinet were rarely opened. Yet there was something in me that knew that drinking would help me not to feel. It was the solution to my problem.

In rural Oregon in the '80s, I had little access to drugs or alcohol, but college gave me freedom. I was admitted to an elite liberal arts school in northern New York state. Thousands of miles away from my family, I thrived. I also drank heavily, but it didn't seem to affect my ability to pull in good grades. I was on the dean's list all but my first term and graduated with all sorts of honors. But drinking was my main interest, and with so many friends over the age of twenty-one, I had alcohol in constant supply.

I had already become an alcoholic early in my college career, and while I didn't see it, others did. I remember going to a hockey game during my freshman year with a friend and her father. I took a thirty-two-ounce plastic mug of beer with me to the game because they were very strict about not selling beer to minors at the hockey rink. I drank the beer as slowly as I could, but by the end of the first period, it was gone. My friend's father could see the panic on my face. He knew that I needed another drink. Sober many years, he looked at me with compassion and said, "It's OK if you need to go." I walked back to the dorm alone so that I could continue drinking.

I was suicidal and depressed during college. Halloween of my freshman year, I broke into the chapel with two friends. One played the piano while I prayed. I didn't know how to process emotion, but being so far from home, surrounded by people who treated me with love and respect, all sorts of feelings started to surface. The worst was the despair. How was I supposed to be OK with what had happened? In that chapel, my friends put their hands on me to pray. I felt a jolt of electricity along with a sense of warmth and love. I didn't have the capacity at that point to feel the old traumas that haunted me, but my friends' love came through. That made an impression on me. Somehow, I could sense that love was the answer. It gave me a tiny bit of hope.

I would have drunk myself to death except that my father died suddenly in April 1995. The last time I saw him was late March. I was visiting his parents in LA before taking a job at an outdoor school in New York state. My father came to town to try to convince me to help him extort a quarter of a million dollars from his parents to buy an office-cleaning business. I was furious. I would not allow him to abuse my grandparents' love for me! When he brought me back from lunch, where he told me about his half-baked plan, I ran into my grandparents' house, slamming the door behind me. I refused to let him in and did not say goodbye. I knew my grandfather had told him that the way you get a business like that is to build it from the ground up, starting by cleaning offices yourself. After I refused to help, my dad thought he'd "show them" by cleaning offices and building the business he wanted. It would have thrilled my grandparents to see him a success by his own labor. Instead of succeeding and being able to gloat, my father had a massive heart attack and died on an office floor in Fresno. He was fifty-two.

I stood at a payphone overlooking Lake George as my mother told me the news. I chose not to go to the funeral, but I was devastated by my father's death. I had dreamed my whole life that someday he'd change and be a father who loved me. My dreams of that "good" father died with him. I needed to escape those feelings like all the others. I drank more than ever.

A man at the outdoor school where I worked suggested to me that I might be an alcoholic. To find out, he proposed that I try to drink no more than a six-pack of beer a night for a week. I did my best. But it took me only ten or fifteen minutes to drink that amount of beer, and I didn't get drunk. It was an intolerable situation, and after only a few days, I returned to my regular drinking pattern.

I moved to Los Angeles, ostensibly to care for my aging grandparents, who were eighty-five at the time. That friend from outdoor school also moved west to San Diego. He eventually got sick of me being drunk all the time and told me not to call him again unless I wanted to go to a twelve step meeting. I had been in LA only a short time; he was my friend. I detoxed alone in my bedroom and went to a meeting a few days later, after the worst of the detox symptoms had subsided. I needed friends more than I needed a drink.

My sobriety was rocky. When I wasn't drinking, I was overwhelmed by agonizing body memories. Even now, after more than twenty years sober, I gratefully still cannot remember much from the years when my father abused me, but my body did not forget. It stored the trauma as sensation. Sometimes, as many as forty times a day, I would feel him—the excruciating pain of being torn apart. Other times, I could feel my father breathing on me, breathing on my neck in a way that made me want to vomit. Often, I would lose track of where I was and be unable to breathe. I would feel the weight of him crushing me. I couldn't speak or scream, just like when I was a little girl.

I went into therapy. It took two years before I could speak the word "incest." I gave my therapist notes to tell her what I wanted to talk about but dissociated before we could make any real headway.

I relapsed a few times in the first two and a half years I tried to get sober. My original sobriety date was November 11, 1995. My current date is June 29, 1998. In those years, the longer I put the bottle down, the more the trauma plagued me. I would lie in bed sometimes, overwhelmed with fear, praying that my father wouldn't come back, disbelieving that he had died. It was unbearable.

A man I met in a twelve step program loved me into sobriety. My dear friend and mentor, Marcel, knew my problem without me ever saying a word. He watched me relapse, eat to blot out my sadness, strike men who spoke to me. He told me that recovery was possible, and he never, ever tried to touch me. I didn't believe him when he said that recovery was possible, but I knew he understood me. I loved him mightily. He was about my father's age, extremely overweight, and a grumpy, misogynistic misanthrope. He was exactly what I dreamed my father could have been if he'd been "good." Marcel was also a bestselling novelist who encouraged me to write. He loved and believed in me when I could not love or believe in myself.

Marcel was diagnosed with an aggressive form of liver cancer in 1998. I was not sober yet. He called me and said he wanted to see me before he died, but I had to be clean because he had "good drugs" in his house that he didn't want me to steal. I loved him and figured I could stay dry longer than he would live. I visited him several times a week, spending hours with him. He told me he wanted to see me get one hundred days sober, and he died when I had 101 or 102 days. I was certain he had held on for me, and that awed me.

Something shifted in me with Marcel's death. The obsession to drink simply left. Some sort of grace came over me, and I was able to stay sober despite the trauma. It is a grace I have continued to experience.

Nine years later, I was sober but miserable. Although I did everything I knew to do—twelve step meetings, psychotherapy, acupuncture, etc.—I remained overwhelmed by trauma. The only relief I had was at my Friday night twelve step meeting. It was near the West LA VA hospital. By this time, veterans were returning from the wars in Iraq and Afghanistan. Although the details of our stories were different, we understood each other. Their struggles with trauma and addiction were the same as mine.

There was one Marine in particular who made a great impression on me. He was twenty-three, and though he wanted a military career, he had been badly wounded in combat. He walked with a cane and had been discharged from the service. He was unable to talk about his experiences in the war. Some days, he sat in his chair and trembled. I asked about his therapy at the VA. He was doing a type of exposure therapy that made him relive the worst experiences of his life. It was difficult for him to tolerate the therapy and stay sober. A few months later, he killed himself. He left behind a wife and an infant child.

I was infuriated by his death. I was miserable in my sobriety, and of the veterans who did not take their own lives, most were unable to get sober. The trauma that held us hostage wasn't our fault and had to be addressed. I changed my focus in graduate school. I knew that, somewhere, there had to be quality treatment for people like us, and I was going to find it. That's how I became an addiction researcher.

After graduate school, I was hired as the research director for a luxury addiction treatment facility owned by a friend of mine. My friend was deeply committed to finding the best therapies to offer at this center, and he gave me carte blanche to identify them. I traveled the world speaking about the relationship between addiction and trauma and connecting with researchers working with all sorts of complementary therapies. The work took years, but I loved it. I learned that there are many effective therapies and that when several are used together, they have a synergistic effect. On its own, none is curative, but together with quality psychotherapy that gets at the root cause of a person's addiction, the results can be extraordinary. At this treatment center, using a protocol that highlighted these complementary therapies, we achieved a success rate that few other treatment programs matched. It was at this treatment facility that I encountered Rock to Recovery.

Sonny Mayo walked into the room where I was having lunch. He has a commanding presence. He's also exceedingly friendly. Sonny immediately introduced himself and said, "Hey, I think I know you from the business." (Before graduate school, I had worked for several years for record labels.) Although I didn't think our paths had crossed in a work setting, I, too, thought he seemed familiar. A colleague of mine told him about my research interests, and he invited me to sit in on his next Rock to Recovery session.

The people in the session were exceptionally ill. None was more than two weeks clean. One woman was so heavily medicated with detox meds that she started to nod off midsession. Sonny calmly walked over and gently pushed her back in her chair when she started to lean too far to the side. He never stopped strumming his guitar. Within an hour, the participants had formed a band they named Raw Oysters and written and performed their song. I was amazed. They weren't going to win a GRAMMY, but the song was good. At the end of their performance, I applauded with genuine appreciation for their effort.

What convinced me that Rock to Recovery was special happened the next morning. I was preparing to give a presentation to everyone in the treatment center's residential program. While they assembled, those who had been in Rock to Recovery sessions the previous day shared their songs with one another. People in treatment for addiction rarely have much to feel proud about, but these people were saying to one another, "Hey, did you hear what Raw Oysters did yesterday?" "No, man, let's listen. You've got to hear the song by our band, Folding Chair."

Sonny contacted me later that day and said that Rock to Recovery was looking for a doctoral-level researcher to conduct an efficacy study on their work. The company's founder, Wes Geer, hoped that by showing in a formal way that Rock to Recovery works, it would be easier to bill insurance for sessions. Although I felt a pull to be part of the group, I declined, explaining that since one of the treatment facilities they serve also paid me, it would be a conflict of interest.

Seven months later, I was laid off. The addiction treatment industry is changing, and research positions like mine, which are not recoupable to insurance, are on the chopping block. My position was cut in order to prepare the business for sale to a large medical group.

I immediately called Sonny and let him know that I no longer had a conflict of interest and would like to discuss the group's research needs. Not long after, Wes and I met by phone.

That's when my life changed.

By this point, I had been sober for nineteen years. I was well known in my field and had had speaking engagements all over the world. I had written a book with the owner of the treatment center where I had worked; that book became an Amazon bestseller. I had also written a well-regarded book of poetry. But I was dissatisfied by the feeling that my life was also very small. Although I used all the complementary therapies I researched, I had not found much relief from the trauma symptoms I endured.

The only thing that really made me feel safe was isolation from men. There were very few middle-aged men in my life, and I rarely allowed myself to be alone with any of them. Most men over the age of twelve or under eighty evoked a flight reaction from me. I could tolerate my friends' husbands for short periods with my friends present, and I was capable of working with a couple of colleagues, but on the whole, men were out. Locked in my room alone, I endured the body memories that still buffeted me. I couldn't risk being assaulted again, and my defense against that, in the absence of alcohol, was to keep all men out.

Despite that decision to keep men out, I took a risk.

Wes and I decided to write a book together—this book. I went to Southern California in April 2018 to conduct interviews. It was a magical collaboration from the start. As part of the project, I interviewed the Rock to Recovery program administrators. Something changed in me. The Rock to Recovery guys seemed to walk right past all my carefully constructed defenses. Although it challenged everything I thought I knew about what was best for me, I began to love them, and I let them love me.

When I got home from the interview tour, I had something of a breakdown. My feelings, long pushed away, were an avalanche. I'd have crying jags in my garage that lasted hours. Often, I would call Wes or Sonny, weeping into the phone that I didn't know what was wrong with me.

Wes, concerned about my well-being and the rapid deterioration of my mental health, suggested action. I wrote songs, like we do in Rock to Recovery sessions, and sent them to Brandon Jordan. I started a somatic experiencing program with Brandon Parkhurst. I went back to twelve step meetings and was pulled kicking and screaming into a morning devotional routine. I had "done the work" before but never with this kind of support and never with a tribe of men.

Working with Brandon Parkhurst was different than any therapeutic relationship I had tried. He walked into those overwhelming feelings with me. In our virtual sessions, feelings would pour out of me the minute his face popped up on the screen. With his help, and with support from the Rock to Recovery program administrators, I began to grow in ways I thought would be closed off to me forever. I was no longer numb. I started to recognize that I could tolerate feelings. It was excruciating. Sometimes, I would hide myself in the closet and sob on the floor because, as a little girl, my closet was the one place I successfully hid from my father, the place where he never found me. Brandon would talk to me in the closet, help me to breathe. I was terrified most of the time, but I could feel.

The guys insisted that I come to the Rock to Recovery 3 benefit concert in Los Angeles. Standing on the red carpet in a circle of men, my brothers, I felt alive. There's an old Polish saying, "Not my circus, not my monkeys." But these guys—a bunch of recovered drug addicts and real-life rock stars—are my circus. I could not love them more, and I know deeply that they love me.

I asked Sonny once, "How did I get in the band when I'm not a musician?" He replied, "I don't know, but you are part of the band." I don't doubt that at all.

Our relationships are a two-way street. I serve as mental health specialist, advisor, and confidant. I am encourager and organizer. I bring snacks to events, help with makeup at photo shoots, and act as stage mom in the most positive sense of the role. The guys buoy and support me, bringing out qualities in me that I didn't believe were safe to share. They help me to be better, to give more, and when I fall short or get dragged down by old memories and trauma, they help me feel safe so that I can move forward again.

I was in San Diego working with Brandon Parkhurst when Christian Heldman died of an overdose in November 2018. I could not believe he died. I sat in my hotel room in a daze. I tried to work but could not. I lapsed in and out of a state of disbelief for more than twenty-four hours until I could get a flight home. Once more, I was numb.

A few days later, in conversation with Phil Bogard, I blurted out, "Christian died." He said, "Yeah, baby, he did." I had so much trouble believing it was true.

I think what hurt me the most is that I am the group's "doctor." Although not a physician, I am often one person the guys turn to with mental health questions and general life problems. I was angry with Christian. What problem could he possibly have had that I could not have helped with? Finance? Romance? Work stress? About the only thing I can't do is magically cure an incurable disease. For just about everything else, I have tremendous resources I can bring to bear on a situation, and all the guys would have lent support.

And yet I understood the tremendous feelings of guilt, shame, and embarrassment Christian must have felt. I feel it in my own struggles with trauma. I don't want to share the feelings I find so loathsome. I fear judgment. For addicts, once the obsession takes hold, we can't always hear the solution, and help becomes something we don't believe is for us.

I asked to sing a U2 song, "Running to Stand Still," at the rock-and-roll memorial Christian's family held. Christian had performed the song a few weeks earlier at Wes' birthday party; it's a song I have always loved.

I was the first performer of the night and was blown away by the number of people in the room. I was backed by Sonny and one of our Orange County program administrators, Clinton. Although I was nervous and grief stricken, I sang my best in Christian's honor. I looked out into the crowd to see Wes recording me with his phone. My guys were there for me as I was for them.

After the performance, I was easing back into numbness. It really was too much, the abruptness and finality of Christian's death coupled with the outpouring of love for him and for me after singing my song. Walking back to my seat, people thanked me and shook my hand. Wes grabbed me in a big bear hug.

As he hugged me, he said, "My hand got a little shaky at the end, but I got the whole thing." He was beaming. My eyes filled with tears.

I pulled back from him a little so I could see his face. "Did I do all right?" I asked. More than anything, I didn't want to embarrass the guys.

"You weren't Beyoncé, but you did good." I could see in his face he was proud of me. I let Wes hug me again.

I saw a picture of us all from the memorial a few days later. I was the only woman in a group of a dozen men. They love me. Most importantly, now I can feel it.

AFTERWORD

Not everyone recovers. Working with more than 2,500 people a month, we hear weekly about former group participants who leave treatment and die. We see their faces in our minds, smiling, laughing, singing. It hurts. But there are a lot of successes, and those are what help us to continue the work. Just as often as we hear about a death, we get notes from participants saying that Rock to Recovery is what led them to stay in treatment instead of quitting. They are sober now. They didn't kill themselves. Attached to the emails are photos and stories of new puppies, marriages, children.

Our work is expanding. Youth services are the fastest-growing area. The experiences of working in a group, finding a community of support, and expressing emotions in a safe and appropriate way are important for children, just as they are for those in treatment for addiction or trauma. One of Rock to Recovery's strategic goals is to bring services to children in the school day, to give them the skills and support they need to prevent addiction and build resiliency before treatment is needed later in life. Let's help our youth develop better mental health before they need to be treated for mental illness. Building community and resiliency is our aim.

We learned during the COVID-19 lockdowns that our programs translate well to the virtual realm. We are now able to provide
virtual music programming to facilities anywhere in the nation.
Further, we have developed coaching and other virtual one-on-one
opportunities so that the general public may access our services.
Our first one-on-one programs have been used by veterans, to sup-
plement the care they receive in their communities. This is an exciting time of growth.

In addition to expanded programming, we have begun working with two groups of researchers. We believe that there is great
value in using music as a therapeutic tool, and we trust that with
published research on Rock to Recovery's work, we will be able to
develop more grant funding. We want anyone who needs it to have
access to therapeutic music programming regardless of ability to
pay.

Finally, a message to each reader. We don't know what drew
you to this book. You may have a problem with substances or know
a veteran who struggles with trauma. You might know one of our
musicians—those featured in this book or one of the other talented program administrators who works with us. You might just
know that on down days, music helps you find a smile. Whatever
your circumstances, however you have reached us, you are wel-
come in our community.

Join us. If you want to bring Rock to Recovery to your organization, we do intensive work through our CI Workshops branch.
Rock to Recovery can be a team- or leadership-building activity
for your company or organization. For these workshops, we fly to
you to serve your group. We work with treatment facilities up and
down the West Coast and in Tennessee with face-to-face groups

and nationally through virtual groups. Our virtual groups are incredibly popular with teens and young adults because we use production software that allows them to program their own music, beyond their ability to play any particular instrument. For those who want individual support, we have coaching services particularly designed to help people early in recovery to build structure and confidence as they lead a sober life outside of a treatment facility. We are a growing organization that has opportunities for you to get the support that you need.

If you need resources, reach out. Even if you require support that we do not provide, we will do what we can to help you find what you are looking for. If you were moved by your experience with a Rock to Recovery program, we want to hear about that too. We want to support you in your growth and success. Contact us through our website or message us through social media.

You are part of Rock to Recovery! Your isolation can end right now. You can let go of feeling shame or remorse. Today is a good day for healing. Join our groups. Come to our concert. Donate to support our nonprofit programs to pay it forward. We are family. It is our distinct honor to help you on your journey of recovery. Right now is the time to open your heart to hope.

And no matter what you face today, please remember, "You're rad!"

ACKNOWLEDGMENTS FROM WES GEER

First, I'd like to thank the people I've been unable to mention. You are all important. Forgive me in advance for omitting your name. I could write three hundred pages and never include everyone who has supported me and this project.

I'd like to thank my mom; Bob Matthews; Sonny Mayo; and my brothers, Alan and Andy, for sowing the earliest seeds of recovery and getting me into treatment.

I'd like to thank Munky and Korn for the opportunity to make this all possible. Without the Korn gig, there is no Rock to Recovery. Thank you to Jim Otell for the secret phone call that saved me from losing the gig.

Thank you to Paul Moen for believing in my vision and giving me the first chance. Thank you to Michelle Gilman for giving me the nudge to take the leap out of Fusion and into this new company. Thank you to Kimiko Miller and our first board members, Kaila Charice, Dave Longridge, and Anthony Christopher.

I'd like to thank the people in the rooms of recovery who shared their experience, strength, and hope for the many hours and years I've been listening. Thank you for carrying the message that transformed my life. Thank you to Ed Spitola and New Found Life for creating a great treatment program and vital lessons. Thank you to Mike, my sponsor in rehab, who came to the facility and took newcomers through the steps. Thank you to all the many people who picked myself and others up from rehab and drove us to meetings. Thank you to Rob M., my first sponsor, and Mitch, my most recent sponsor.

Thank you to all the guys in Hed, my management team, and everyone who supported me during my wildest, darkest times.

Thank you to all the guys in Rock to Recovery, past and present, who brought their heart and passion to our shared mission.

Thank you to Tony Jasso and Marsha Gonzales for our first opportunity to work with vets.

Thank you to Constance as my VP, PhD, doc, and coauthor.

Thank you to the giant group of people who help us pull off our shows like Billy Morrison, Franky Perez, Mike Ness, Wayne Kramer, Corey Taylor, Moby, Katey Sagal, Bailey and everyone at the Fonda, Kir and Bobby Danelski, Galina, Priscilla Vento, and all of our current board members.

Thank you to Joey Darby, Kathleen Bigsby, Matt Feehery, everyone at Foundations Recovery Network, and all of our other amazing sponsors for the events.

Thank you to Brad Zell and QSC, Brad Delava and Apogee, everyone at Izotope, Davida and Shure Microphones, Rode Mics, and all the gear companies that have supported us along the way.

Thank you to every clinical director, program director, support staff member, and everyone at all the treatment centers we've had the honor of working with.

ACKNOWLEDGMENTS FROM CONSTANCE SCHARFF

The journey of writing this book began for me when Mindy Johnson introduced me to Sonny Mayo while we were having lunch at Cliffside Malibu, overlooking the Pacific Ocean. It has started and ended as a dream.

Thank you to Mindy for advocating for me, Delphine Robertson for having my back, and Richard Taite for creating a job for me to learn from some of the world's pre-eminent researchers. My years in service to Cliffside prepared me to write this book.

Thank you to Sonny for seeing something extraordinary in me and introducing me to Wes. Wes has been a wonderful collaborative partner. I am grateful to be on this path with both of you.

Frances Bowdery set up the interviews for this book. Thank you to her and the thirty people I interviewed for this project. I am honored to have spent an hour or two with each of you. Your stories are an inspiration! Mike and Carol, thank you both for allowing me to stay with you while I conducted the interviews, for the use of the car, and for supporting me as I took in the difficult stories people had to share.

Thank you to Brian "Head" Welch for writing the foreword. Your support is a gift.

Thank you, too, to the Rock to Recovery program administrators. It is your work that brings light to thousands of suffering souls each and every month. Of course, we could not do this work without our program partners, who open the doors of recovery and walk with their clients. Nor would our work be possible without Rock to Recovery's donors and sponsors. You provide the resources to bring music to people who could not otherwise afford it. Our board of directors are the stewards who help shepherd these resources so that we can reach more people every year.

We appreciate Sam Henrie and everyone at Wheatmark for their support in helping us publish this book. We also thank Samantha Bennington and the Around the Way Publishing team for taking on this project.

I would like to thank Duncan and the people in the "rooms" who are my support. Roby Blecker, your editorial efforts were a tremendous help. I appreciate your patience with all the fits and starts in this project. Meg, Leigh, Allison, Linde, and the "cowgirls," where would I be without your courage, particularly when it comes to men and mice? Dr. Chang provides me with acupuncture to sedate or uplift as needed. Piper Sample, I know the term "therapist" doesn't technically apply to you, but the work we do together has had more positive impact on me than anything else I have tried. Thank you for walking with me in the darkest spaces.

ABOUT THE AUTHORS

Wes Geer has been a professional musician for over twenty-five years. He first gained success as a founding member of Jive Records artists Hed PE and later as touring guitarist with the legendary band Korn. After completing his career as a touring musician, Wes founded Rock to Recovery, an innovative music program that harnesses the healing energy of music through songwriting, playing as a band, and recording.

Constance Scharff, PhD is an internationally recognized speaker and author on the topics of addiction recovery and mental health. She currently serves Rock to Recovery as VP Business Development. Previously, Dr. Scharff was Senior Addiction Research Fellow and Director of Addiction Research for a luxury addiction treatment center based in Malibu, California. She is the 2019 recipient of St. Lawrence University's Sol Feinstone Humanitarian Award, honoring her service to and advocacy for those suffering from mental illness, trauma, and addiction.

ENDNOTES

1   R. Dunbar, K. Kaskatis, I. MacDonald, and V. Barra, "Performance of Music Elevates Pain Threshold and Positive Affect: Implications for the Evolutionary Function of Music," *Evolutionary Psychology*, 2012, 10(4), 688-702.

2   C. Grape, M. Sandgren, L. O. Hansson, M. Ericson and T. Theorell, "Does Singing Promote Well-Being?: An Empirical Study of Professional and Amateur Singers During a Singing Lesson," *Physiological & Behavioral Science*, 2002, (38), 65-74.

3   C. J. Murrock, "Music and Mood," in A. V. Clark (Ed.), *Psychology of Moods*, (Hauppauge, NY: Nova Science Publishers, 2005), pp. 141-155.

4   Compiled data from the Centers for Disease Control and Prevention (CDC), Retrieved 2020, https://www.cdc.gov/alcohol/fact-sheets/alcohol-use.htm, and National Institute on Drug Abuse (NIDA), https://www.drugabuse.gov/related-topics/trends-statistics/overdose-death-rates.

5   "Provisional drug Overdose Death Counts," Centers for Disease Control and Prevention, 2021, https://www.cdc.gov/nchs/nvss/vsrr/drug-overdose-data.htm.

6   From the Surgeon General's November 2016 report as

reported by *USA Today*, 2016, https://www.usatoday.com/ story/news/nation-now/2016/11/17/surgeon-general-1-7-us-face-substance-addiction/93993474/.

7　"10 Percent of US Adults Have Drug Use Disorder at Some Point in Their Lives," National Institutes of Health, https:// www.nih.gov/news-events/news-releases/10-percent-us-adults-have-drug-use-disorder-some-point-their-lives.

8　"Drug Overdose: Overdose trends," Drug Policy Alliance, 2021, https://drugpolicy.org/issues/drug-overdose.

9　"The First Count of Fentanyl Deaths in 2016: Up 540 Percent in Three Years," *New York Times*. September 2, 2017, https:// www.nytimes.com/interactive/2017/09/02/upshot/fentan-yl-drug-overdose-deaths.html.

10　"Drug Overdose Deaths Reach an All-Time High," CNN, December 18, 2015, https://www.cnn.com/2015/12/18/ health/drug-overdose-deaths-2014/index.html.

11　"Overdose Deaths Appear to Rise Amid Coronavirus Pandem-ic in US," NBC, October 20, 2020, https://www.nbcnews. com/health/health-news/overdose-deaths-appear-rise-amid-coronavirus-pandemic-u-s-n1244024.

12　"Pain Management and the Opioid Epidemic: Balancing Soci-etal and Individual Benefits and Risks of Prescription Opioid Use: Trends in Opioid Use, Harms, and Treatment," National Center for Biotechnology Information, US National Library of Medicine, July 2017, https://www.ncbi.nlm.nih.gov/ books/NBK458661/.

13　"CDC Fact Sheet," *New York Times*, September 2017, https:// www.cdc.gov/alcohol/fact-sheets/alcohol-use.htm Reported in the. https://www.nytimes.com/interactive/2017/09/02/

upshot/fentanyl-drug-overdose-deaths.html CDC Morbidity and Mortality Weekly Report. https://www.cdc.gov/mmwr/preview/mmwrhtml/mm6450a3.htmaandemic in U.S.

14 Josh Katz, "The First Count of Fentanyl Deaths in 2016: Up 540 percent in Three Years," *New York Times*, September 2, 2017, https://www.nytimes.com/interactive/2017/09/02/upshot/fentanyl-drug-overdose-deaths.html.

15 "America Addicted," PBS, October, 2017, https://www.pbs.org/newshour/features/america-addicted/.

16 Karen Kaplan, "Opioid Overdose Deaths Are Still Rising in Nearly Every Segment of the Country, CDC Says," *Los Angeles Times*, March 29, 2018, http://www.latimes.com/science/sciencenow/la-sci-sn-opioid-overdose-deaths-20180329-htmlstory.html.

17 Sandra Garrido, Felicity A. Baker, Jane W. Davidson, Grace Moore and Steve Wasserman, "Music and Trauma: The Relationship Between Music, Personality, and Coping Style," *Frontiers in Psychology*, July 10, 2015, https://doi.org/10.3389/fpsyg.2015.00977.

18 "Keep Your Brain Young with Music," Johns Hopkins Medicine, 2021, https://www.hopkinsmedicine.org/health/wellness-and-prevention/keep-your-brain-young-with-music#:~:text=%E2%80%9CIf%20you%20want%20to%20keep,%2C%20mental%20alertness%2C%20and%20memory.

19 "Improving the Quality of Mental Health Care for Veterans: Lessons from RAND Research," Rand Corporation, 2019, https://www.rand.org/pubs/research_briefs/RB10087.html.

20 Jeffrey M. Jones, "Majority of US Veterans Say Access to VA

Care Difficult," Gallup, July, 2014, http://news.gallup.com/poll/172055/majority-veterans-say-access-care-difficult.aspx.

21 "Removing Barriers to Mental Health Services for Veterans," American Public Health Association, 2014, https://www.apha.org/policies-and-advocacy/public-health-policy-statements/policy-database/2015/01/28/14/51/removing-barriers-to-mental-health-services-for-veterans.

22 Ronald D. Hester, "Lack of Access to Mental Health Services Contributing to the High Suicide Rates Among Veterans, *International Journal of Mental Health Systems,* 11, 47, 2017, https://doi.org/10.1186/s13033-017-0154-2.

23 Michael H. Thaut, "Neuromusicology." *AccessScience,* 2020, https://doi.org/10.1036/1097-8542.449970.

24 Tom Barnes, "Science Shows How Musicians' Brains Are Different from Everybody Else's," *Mic,* August 13, 2014, https://www.mic.com/articles/96150/science-shows-how-musicians-brains-are-different-from-everybody-elses.

25 Vinoo Alluri, Petri Toiviainen, Iballa Burunat, Marina Kliuchko, Peter Vuust and Elvira Brattico, "Connectivity Patterns During Music Listening: Evidence for Action-Based Processing in Musicians," *Hum. Brain Mapp,* 38, 2955-2970, 2017, https://doi.org/10.1002/hbm.23565.

26 Michel Habib and Mireille Besson, "What Do Music Training and Musical Experience Teach Us About Brain Plasticity?" *Music Perception,* 26(3), 279-285, 2009, https://doi.org/10.1525/mp.2009.26.3.279.

27 Valorie N. Salimpoor, Mitchel Benovoy, Kevin Larcher, Alain Dagher, and Robert J. Zatorre, "Anatomically Distinct

Dopamine Release During Anticipating and Experience of Peak Emotion to Music," *Nature Neuroscience*, 2011, https://www.nature.com/articles/nn.2726.

28 Patricia Izbicki, "Your Brain Will Thank You for Being a Musician: Here Are Five Reasons Why," *Scientific American*, 2020, https://blogs.scientificamerican.com/observations/your-brain-will-thank-you-for-being-a-musician/.

29 Jason Keeler, Edward A. Roth, Brittany L. Neuser, John M. Spitsbergen, Daniel J. M. Waters, and John-Mary Vianney, "The Neurochemistry and Social Flow of Singing: Bonding and Oxytocin," *Frontiers in Human Neuroscience* (9), 518, September 23, 2015, https://doi.org/10.3389/fnhum.2015.00518.

30 Patrick Edward Kennedy, "The Relationship Between Prosocial Music and Helping Behaviour and Its Mediators: An Irish College Sample," *Journal of European Psychology Students* (4), 1-15, 2013, https://jeps.efpsa.org/articles/abstract/10.5334/jeps.av/.

Made in the USA
Las Vegas, NV
15 July 2021

26497576R00157